Ludwig Bemelmans

Twayne's United States Authors Series

Ruth K. MacDonald, Editor

Bay Path College

TUSAS 665

LUDWIG BEMELMANS
Courtesy of Madeleine Bemelmans

Ludwig Bemelmans

Jacqueline Fisher Eastman

Birmingham, Alabama

Twayne Publishers
An Imprint of Simon & Schuster Macmillan
New York

Prentice Hall International
London Mexico City New Delhi Singapore Sydney Toronto

Twayne's United States Authors Series No. 665
Ludwig Bemelmans

Jacqueline Fisher Eastman

Twayne Publishers
An Imprint of Simon & Schuster Macmillan
1633 Broadway
New York, NY 10019

Library of Congress Cataloging-in-Publication Data
Eastman, Jackie Fisher.
    Ludwig Bemelmans / Jackie Fisher Eastman.
        p.   cm.— (Twayne's United States authors series ; 665)
    Includes bibliographical references and index.
    ISBN 0-8057-4535-1 (cloth : alk. paper)
        1. Bemelmans, Ludwig, 1898–1962—Criticism and interpretation.
    2. Children's stories, American—History and criticism.   3. Humorous
    stories, American—History and criticism.   I. Title.   II. Series:
    Twayne's United States authors series ; TUSAS 665.
    PS3503.E475Z65   1996
    818'.5209—dc20   96-20001
                                                            CIP

The paper used in this publication meets the minimum requirements of American
National Standard for Information Sciences—Permanence of Paper for Printed Library
Materials, ANSI Z39.48-1984. ∞™

10 9 8 7 6 5 4 3 2 1 (hc)

Printed in the United States of America.

To Bob, Alex, and Sarah—my so dear family—
for support, love, and patience.

Contents

Preface   *ix*
Acknowledgments   *xiii*
Chronology   *xvii*

Chapter One
A Multifaceted Career   1

Chapter Two
Children's Books for Children: The Massee Influence   20

Chapter Three
Madeline and the Sequels: The Making of a Classic Series   50

Chapter Four
Children's Books for Adults   89

Chapter Five
Madeline: Modern More than Fifty Years Later   116

Notes and References   *125*
Selected Bibliography   *137*
Index   *145*

Preface

More than 50 years ago, Ludwig Bemelmans published *Madeline,* his fifth children's book in as many years. An instant success with critics and readers of all ages, the work and its successors continue to thrive in a variety of formats today, clearly having achieved "classic" status. Yet as popular as the series continues to be, there has been until this time no book-length study devoted to these works and to the other children's publications of this multitalented author.

This study argues first of all that a good deal of *Madeline's* success is the result of the book's ability to appeal to both children and adults, a fact noted at the time. Following *Madeline's* 1939 appearance in *Life* magazine, Bemelmans first published nearly every one of his children's works in adult magazines—*Town and Country, Good Housekeeping, Holiday, McCall's, Woman's Day,* and *Mademoiselle.* In some cases this resulted in flawed children's books; for the *Madeline* series, however, it meant increased readership for a work uniquely attractive to readers both young and old.

Wanting to enjoy life's finest comforts, Bemelmans had every intention of making children's books a highly profitable trade; thus, he promoted *Madeline* and his other works in many ways besides the dual magazine/book presentations, using such tactics as gallery sales of the original artwork, lavish promotional campaigns, and media formats. In the tradition of John Newbery, he was well aware of the value of the toy accompanying the book as a means of increasing sales, and would almost certainly have approved of the plethora of Madeline dolls and other toys that are currently on the market.

Immigrating to New York in 1914 when only a teenager, Bemelmans first entered the trade of his European relatives, the hotel and restaurant business. Although his experiences in kitchens and parlors provided countless anecdotes for the humorous magazine articles and books that were to come, they did not in themselves offer creative fulfillment. Thus, after some 15 years, Bemelmans struck out on his own as an artist, only to flounder during the depression era until Viking editor May Massee "discovered" him and offered him a chance in children's book publishing.

For the next 30 years, Massee and Bemelmans enjoyed a highly fruitful working relationship. In preparing the current study, I have been the first to utilize the files of their correspondence at the Viking Press (now

Penguin USA). These letters show Bemelmans's growth from an eager-to-please newcomer, struggling to satisfy the supportive editor, into a worldly artist, confident of his own style. They show, too, that although Bemelmans and Massee did not agree on every point, their relationship was warm and full of mutual respect.

In Chapter 1 I have outlined Bemelmans's career, including his adult writings as well as his works for children. The second, third, and fourth chapters look at his children's books up to *Madeline,* the *Madeline* series, and the post-*Madeline* books, respectively. Finally, in the last chapter I examine the many ways in which *Madeline* continues to be modern, for the multitude of similarities between *Madeline* and other works for children more than 50 years after its publication is truly remarkable. In some cases it would seem that *Madeline*'s tremendous popularity may even have exerted an influence for change in picturebook norms, an idea pursued by Zohar Shavit with respect to other children's works in her book *Poetics of Children's Literature.*

As an author/illustrator, Bemelmans was not only well known for his works for children; his humorous autobiographical writings for adults were also very popular. Month after month, his illustrated articles detailing the curiosities and ironies of subjects such as hotel life, travel, high society, and fatherhood appeared in national publications. Year after year, many of these periodical articles found their way into hardback anthologies and novels. Since 1985, when Viking published the anthology *Tell Them It Was Wonderful,* there has been a renaissance of interest in these writings. My Bibliography lists not only Bemelmans's works for children, but also all of his titles for adults, including recent reprints.

Research on Bemelmans has until very recently been immensely complicated, and this is so for many reasons. For instance, some of his early magazine articles are not listed in the standard references; thus "Fifi" and "Nosegay"—the magazine version of *Rosebud*—were found in *Town and Country* through a combination of hunch and a scholar's version of pounding the pavement—going through one bound volume after another. One of the most difficult challenges of all was finding Bemelmans's first comic strip, "Thrilling Adventures of Count Bric a Brac." Without giving a date, Bemelmans mentions this strip in the sketch entitled "The Old Ritz," saying that he wrote it for the *World.* After I had looked for many months, a librarian suggested contacting Bill Blackbeard of the San Francisco Academy of Comic Arts. Blackbeard not only knew the strip, he had insights to share and was happy to mail me 13 examples from the *Milwaukee Journal,* where the "Count" had also appeared. Another one of my treasures, purchased from a children's book dealer, is the original *Madeline's Christmas*—a tiny book insert—which first appeared in *McCall's* in 1956. Not only was finding material in periodicals and newspapers difficult at times, collecting books by Bemelmans could also be challenging, as most of them are out of print. Most frustrating of all during the seven years or so that I was working on Bemelmans was the absence of a bibliography of his enormous and varied outpouring. Finally, in 1993, Murray Pomerance published his highly useful volume, the product of 10 years of research. In the past several months this work has helped me put final touches on mine.

Ludwig Bemelmans—children's book author, adult humorist, and gallery artist. Bon vivant and traveler. The scholar's work on Bemelmans is only just beginning, I would venture to state. Madeleine Bemelmans warned me more than once in letters not to believe everything her husband had said or that had been written about him: "Much of what Ludwig wrote or said in interviews was a blend of fact and fiction—not for purposes of deception but to make a good story."[1] For example, this study has uncovered two different versions, each told by Bemelmans himself, of the precise inspiration for the rescue scene in *Madeline's Rescue.* I have also corrected Bemelmans's statement that *Madeline* sat "in a drawer for five years"[2] after he first wrote it. Nothing could be further from the truth; Simon & Schuster took it promptly after May Massee turned it down. Despite painstaking efforts, I suspect that future studies will similarly uncover mistakes reproduced in my own work. Bemelmans's comments when asked how closely he stuck to the truth in his autobiographical writing suggest some of the problem: "Often what I write is true. But it is almost a game. 'This,' an editor will say, 'is fiction.' 'No,' I answer, 'that is true.' 'But this part certainly is true,' he'll say. 'No, that is fiction.'"[3]

So it is that one of the most gratifying pieces of correspondence I received during the course of this project was from Madeleine Bemelmans. After graciously complimenting an article which I published in *Children's Literature,* she noted that "Ludwig's mother—who was so distressed by his poor performance at school—would have been proud to know that his books and pictures merited scholarly attention."[4] Despite his early failures, Bemelmans left a body of work that would make any mother proud. His legacy of delight will enchant readers— and occupy scholars—for years to come.

Acknowledgments

I would like to thank Penguin Books USA Inc. for permission to quote from the following:

From the text and page 33 illustration of *Madeline* by Ludwig Bemelmans. Copyright 1939 by Ludwig Bemelmans, renewed © 1967 by Madeleine Bemelmans and Barbara Bemelmans Marciano. Used by permission of Viking Penguin, a division of Penguin Books USA Inc.

From *Madeline's Rescue* by Ludwig Bemelmans. Copyright 1951, 1953 by Ludwig Bemelmans, renewed © 1979, 1981 by Madeleine Bemelmans and Barbara Marciano. Used by permission of Viking Penguin, a division of Penguin Books USA Inc.

From *Madeline and the Bad Hat* by Ludwig Bemelmans. Copyright © 1956 by Ludwig Bemelmans. Used by permission of Viking Penguin, a division of Penguin Books USA Inc.

From *Madeline and the Gypsies* by Ludwig Bemelmans. Copyright © 1958, 1959 by Ludwig Bemelmans, renewed © 1986, 1987 by Madeleine Bemelmans and Barbara Bemelmans. Used by permission of Viking Penguin, a division of Penguin Books USA Inc.

From *Madeline in London* by Ludwig Bemelmans. Copyright © 1961 by Ludwig Bemelmans; renewed copyright © 1989 by Madeleine Bemelmans and Barbara Bemelmans. Used by permission of Viking Penguin, a division of Penguin Books USA Inc.

From *Madeline's Christmas* by Ludwig Bemelmans. Copyright © 1956 by Ludwig Bemelmans, renewed © 1984 by Madeleine Bemelmans and Barbara B. Marciano. Used by permission of Viking Penguin, a division of Penguin Books USA Inc.

Page 53 illustration from *The Golden Basket* by Ludwig Bemelmans. Copyright 1935 by Ludwig Bemelmans, renewed © 1964 by Madeleine and Barbara Bemelmans. Used by permission of Viking Penguin, a division of Penguin Books USA Inc.

Page 47 illustration from *Quito Express* by Ludwig Bemelmans. Copyright 1938 by Ludwig Bemelmans, renewed © 1966 by Madeleine Bemelmans and Barbara Bemelmans Marciano. Used by permission of Viking Penguin, a division of Penguin Books USA Inc.

I would like to thank International Creative Management for permission to reprint the following:

 Illustration from *The Castle Number Nine* (New York: Viking, 1937).

Illustration from *Hansi* (New York: Viking, 1934).

I would like to thank Mrs. Madeleine Bemelmans for permission to reprint the following:

Illustration from "Madeline in London," *Holiday,* August 1961.

I would like to thank the Continuum Publishing Group for permission to reprint "Max and Moritz" (1865), trans. Walter Arndt, in *Wilhelm Busch and Others: German Satirical Writings,* ed. Dieter P. Lotze and Volkmar Sander. © 1984 by the Continuum Publishing Group.

I would like to thank warmly the following: Madeleine Bemelmans for timely and careful answers to my many questions and for permission to quote from Bemelmans's letters at Viking Press and from other unpublished materials in the New York Public Library and the May Massee Collection at Emporia State University; Michael Patrick Hearne for his summer course in the history of picture books at Columbia University School of Library Service, for the suggestion to use the Bemelmans material at Viking Press, and for helping me locate the *Hansi* dummy and other materials in the New York Public Library system; Talladega College for the Lilly Foundation grant that facilitated this research; Mark Zadrozny, for his commitment to this project; Ruth K. MacDonald, my editor, for faith in me and kind words; Barbara Sutton, Twayne copyeditor, for patient, precise, and reassuring answers to many many questions; Mary Reed, Twayne production editorial assistant, for cheerful competence; assistants at Viking Press; Dr. Robert Halli of the University of Alabama English Department for guiding this research in its earliest stages; Dr. Roberta Long of the University of Alabama at Birmingham School of Education for information about current reading theory and especially for enthusiastic encouragement; Dr. Shirley Musgrave of the University of Alabama Department of Art Education for hours of coaching in how to look at and describe Bemelmans's paintings; Dr. Richard Thames of the University of Montevallo for help with German; Bill Blackbeard, Director of the San Francisco Academy of Comic Arts for sending me original copies of "Count Bric a Brac"; Drusilla's Books for searching and finding many of the volumes I needed; Bernard Wiseman for reminiscing; and Dr. James Lynch, D.V.M., for help in identifying Fifi's boyfriend.

I also extend my gratitude to many wonderful librarians, especially Richard Bleiler, Tinker Dunbar, and Gordon Dunkin of Mervyn Stern Library, the University of Alabama at Birmingham; Mary Bogan of the William Allen White Library, Emporia State University; Helen Fleming, St. Paul Public Library; Julanne M. Good, Children's Collection, St. Louis Public Library; Tom Haslett, University of Montevallo Library; Karen Nelson Hoyle, Curator, Kerlan Collection, University of Minnesota; Angeline Moscatt, Central Children's Center, New York Public Library, Donnell Library Center; Jane Rohlfing, Special Collections, Rare Books Room, University of Colorado at Boulder; Angie Schatz, Hoover Public Library, Birmingham; Linda Sheikh, Huffman High School, Birmingham.

Finally, personal thanks to my mother, Dorothy Fisher, who first taught me to delight in Bemelmans. To my husband, Bob, who has helped in every way conceivable—applying his genius to broken sentences, teaching for me when I had a deadline to meet, and above all, valuing my work. To Alex, who made me a masterful watercolor copy of the cover of *Sunshine* and was always quietly there for me. To Sarah, who taught herself to read on *Madeline*, lugged my lunchbox computer through the subways of New York and up the elevator to Viking Press every day for a week, and helped find Bemelmans articles at a quarter apiece in the bound periodicals section of the St. Louis Public Library.

Chronology

Ludwig Bemelmans is born on 30 April in Meran, Austria (now Merano, Italy), to Frances Fischer and Lambert Bemelmans.

ca. 1904 With his mother, leaves Gmunden and moves to Regensburg, Germany.

1914 Arrives in New York.

1918 Becomes a naturalized U.S. citizen.

1926 Comic strip, "Thrilling Adventures of Count Bric a Brac."

1929 Leaves hotel business just before Depression begins.

ca. 1930–32 Meets May Massee.

1933 "Noodles the Trained Seal" in *Saturday Evening Post*.

1934 First book, *Hansi*. Marries Madeleine Freund 23 November. Hitler becomes absolute dictator in Germany.

1935 Broadway opening of *Noah's Ark*. "Silly Willy" cartoons begin in March. Travels with Madeleine to Belgium for material. Leaves Germany, unable to work.

1936 *The Golden Basket*. Daughter, Barbara, born.

1937 *The Golden Basket* wins Newbery Honor Award. Visits South America twice collecting material for *Quito Express* and other works. His first adult book, *My War with the United States*. *Noodle* (illustrations). *The Castle Number Nine*.

1938 Accident on Île d'Yeu off France places him in hospital, where he meets an inspiration for the character Madeline. Rehearses *Good Hunting* but does not appear in its (November) opening.

1939 *Madeline* (Simon & Schuster; first book with a publisher other than Viking). France enters World War II.

1940 *Madeline* wins Caldecott Honor Award. *Fifi*.

1941   *The Donkey Inside.*

1942   *Rosebud.*

1944   First novel, *Now I Lay Me Down To Sleep.*

1945   *Yolanda and the Thief* (MGM).

1947   *A Tale of Two Glimps.* Completes murals on wall in what is now called the Bemelmans Bar in the Hotel Carlyle.

1950   *Sunshine: A Story about the City of New York.*

1951   *Sunshine: A Story about the City of New York* wins *New York Herald Tribune* Spring Book Award. "Madeline's Rescue" appears in *Good Housekeeping.*

1952   *The Happy Place.*

1953   *Madeline's Rescue* and *Father, Dear Father.*

1954   *Madeline's Rescue* wins Caldecott Award. *The High World.*

1955   *Parsley.* "Madeline's Christmas" appears in *Good Housekeeping;* same story, called *Madeline's Christmas in Texas,* is published for Neiman Marcus.

1956   "Madeline's Christmas," book insert for *McCall's.*

1957   *Madeline and the Bad Hat.*

1958   Viking purchases the rights to the original *Madeline* from Simon & Schuster. "Madeline and the Gypsies" appears in *McCall's.*

1959   *Madeline and the Gypsies.* "Bemelmans' New York" opens at the Museum of the City of New York.

1960   *Welcome Home!*

1961   "Madeline in London" appears in *Holiday. Madeline in London.*

1962   Bemelmans dies in New York City 1 October. *Marina.*

1964   *La Bonne Table.*

1985   *Tell Them It Was Wonderful* and *Madeline's Christmas.*

1993   *Mad about Madeline: The Complete Tales* and *Ludwig Bemelmans: A Bibliography.*

Chapter One

A Multifaceted Career

Ludwig Bemelmans, as his Viking editor and friend May Massee wrote, "never stops working and he never stops learning."[1] Bemelmans created the enduring children's classic *Madeline*, as well as five sequels, and 13 other books for children. He won the Newbery Honor Award, the Caldecott Honor Award, and the Caldecott Award. In his lifetime he was equally appreciated as the author of humorous illustrated stories and articles for adults, some of which are currently being reissued; in fact, he is regarded by *The Dictionary of American Biography* as "one of the most distinguished figures in the long line of American humorists."[2] He wrote seven novels and a movie screenplay. He exhibited regularly at art galleries, and he decorated walls of studios and restaurants. Early in his career he decided that he wanted to enjoy life's material comforts in abundance; thus he marketed his products with tremendous creativity and energy, getting double and triple exposure from most projects. Through his many activities, he became a public figure, well-known for his talents, his tastes, his geniality, and his humor.

Beginnings

Ludwig Bemelmans was born on 30 April 1898, in Meran, Austria (now Merano, Italy).[3] His Belgian father, Lambert, was an artist; his mother, Frances Fischer, was the daughter of a wealthy Bavarian brewer. When he was very young, Bemelmans's family moved to Gmunden, where his father had inherited a hotel known as the Golden Ship and other property; here the child passed his days under the attentive eye of a loving French governess. When he was six, Bemelmans's idyllic life came to an abrupt end when his father ran off with the governess.[4]

Bemelmans then moved with his mother to the home of her father in Regensburg, Germany, on the Danube. Bemelmans's wife, Madeleine, notes that although Bemelmans had not had a particularly good relationship with his father before he left, he nevertheless suffered from his absence. A letter he wrote not long before his death suggests the emptiness of his childhood: "I have forgotten so much of youth and much of it was not experienced. In me a whole portion of it is missing—it is like a floor in a house where there is no furniture" (in M. Bemelmans, xvi).

Failing scholastically in more than one setting, Bemelmans finally went as a young teenager to work for his uncle Hans, who owned a string of Tyrolean resort hotels. The exact reason for his departure for America is debated. In "Lausbub," first published in *Life Class* in 1938, Bemelmans says that as a result of "a very serious offense" in one of these hotels, his uncle gave him the choice of going to a reform school on a German merchant marine training ship or leaving for America.[5] In a *New York Times Book Review* in 1941, Bemelmans wrote more about the offense, describing an encounter with a "vicious" headwaiter: "He wanted to beat me with a heavy leather whip and I told him that if he hit me I would shoot him. He hit me and I shot him in the abdomen. For some time it seemed he would die. He didn't." Nevertheless, Bemelmans continues, the police forced upon his family the unpleasant choice of sending him "either to a reform school or to America" (Van Gelder, 2). Writing 10 years later, in 1951, Henry C. Pitz reported both the "America or a reform school" version of the story along with yet another: Bemelmans came to America because Uncle Hans wanted him to learn modern American techniques of hotelkeeping.[6] And most recently, Madeleine Bemelmans has written without elaboration, "I don't believe he ever shot a headwaiter."[7] Whatever the immediate cause, in 1914, at the age of 16, speaking very little English, Bemelmans arrived in New York City. Before boarding in Rotterdam, at the urging of the boat's captain, he traded in the two pistols he had purchased to fight off the Indians, and wound up with three pocket knives and 12 pairs of scissors.[8] His father failed to meet him, and he spent Christmas Eve on Ellis Island.

For the next twenty-some years, until his mid-thirties, Bemelmans worked primarily in hotels and restaurants, in positions ranging from busboy to part owner. Enlisting in the U.S. Army in 1917, he left New York City, serving for a time as an attendant in a government mental ward. In 1918 he became a U.S. citizen.

In 1926 Bemelmans finally realized for a brief time a dream of becoming a comic strip artist, producing "Thrilling Adventures of Count Bric a Brac" for six months for the *New York World*. Unfortunately, this happy experience was short-lived. In "The Old Ritz," Bemelmans says that he was fired from the *World* because of complaints about his strip and because after six months no syndicate had picked it up.[9] More than a decade later, in a magazine interview, he noted that readers "didn't like the Count or the poetry he recited."[10] Yet inasmuch as his strip appeared in the *Milwaukee Journal,*[11] it seems a bit misleading to say that no syndicate had picked it up. Bill Blackbeard, director of the San Francisco Academy of Comic Arts, has stated that he doubts Bemelmans was actually fired unless he was asking for a raise, noting further that in his opinion the strip was one of the best of the 1920s.[12] For whatever reasons, Bemelmans was soon back at the hotel where "it was a bitter time" ("Old Ritz," 158).

A couple of years later, in September 1929, disgusted with the overly secure, unfulfilled person he saw in the mirror, Bemelmans again left the hotel business to make his way as an artist. His timing was terrible; two weeks later the stock market crashed, and "nobody bought any pictures, nobody had any money" ("Old Ritz," 159).

The 1930s: Rapid Rise to Fame

In the early 1930s, while Bemelmans was freelancing for an advertising studio, things took a sudden turn for the better. A lithographer friend, Mark Liddell, brought Viking children's book editor May Massee to his rooms on Eighth Street. Seeing the scenes of the Tyrol and the imaginative furniture that the homesick artist had painted on the walls and window shades of his apartment, Massee asked Bemelmans to do a children's book using the same kinds of images.[13] The resulting *Hansi* (1934), a sensitive evocation of his own memories of childhood, launched his career. In the same year, on 23 November 1934, Bemelmans married Madeleine Freund, the daughter of a Westchester banker, at the Frenchtown, New Jersey, home of fellow children's book artist, Kurt Wiese.

Soon after marriage, Bemelmans gave up his part ownership of the Hapsburg House restaurant, and early in 1935, he and Madeleine departed for Belgium, where he acquired material for his next book. *The Golden Basket,* a Newbery Honor Award winner, appeared in 1936, the same year in which their daughter, Barbara, was born.[14] Next came the witty *The Castle Number Nine* (1937), the illustrations for Munro Leaf's popular *Noodle* (1937), and, following trips to South America, *Quito Express* (1938). This intense period of productivity in children's literature was capped with the creation of *Madeline* (1939).

For young readers, Bemelmans was creating not only books during this period but a weekly comic strip as well. Featuring a trained seal, "Silly Willy" appeared in *Young America,* a weekly magazine for schoolchildren. According to bibliographer Murray Pomerance, Bemelmans produced these short cartoons with rhyming text for about two years, beginning with the first issue on 8 March 1935.[15]

Within three years after he began publishing books for children, Bemelmans entered the field of adult literature with books of illustrated verbal sketches. The first of these was *My War with the United States* (1937), a translation of the moving and humorous diary he had written in German during his World War I military service some 20 years before. The next work, *Life Class* (1938), was based on his many years of experiences in hotels. Critics began appreciating him as humorist and satirist, and one noted that he "writes as perfect an equivalent of his ingenuously sophisticated drawings as James Thurber does of his."[16] *Small Beer,* a collection of 10 short stories and sketches, appeared the same year as *Madeline* (1939).

Bemelmans's prolific outpourings for magazines constitute what, for a less energetic mortal, might have been the output of an entire career. In many ways, of course, his careers as book and magazine humorist overlapped, for he frequently compiled books from pieces that had appeared earlier in periodicals. In both areas of publication, one of his most pervasive public personas was the professional traveler. As early as 1936, he treated the readers of *Vogue* to a witty and informative illustrated report on *The Golden Basket* trip to Bruges.[17] Likewise, the trips to South America yielded articles for *House Beautiful,* the *New Yorker,* and *Town and Country.* Bemelmans's travelogues were appealing not only because of their blend of information and humor, but also because of the accompanying pictures. As *Saturday Review* critic Lee Rogow wrote of Bemelmans in the 1950s, "How useful a thing it is for the writer to be an artist!"[18]

As a result of his writings for children and adults, Bemelmans quickly began to achieve fame; for instance, he was recognized as one of 10 "Stars Breaking Through" in *Vogue* for August 1939—in the company of figures such as Abbott and Costello, Oscar Levant, Greer Garson, Katherine Anne Porter, and Antoine de Saint-Exupéry. The article described him as "the thoroughly unpredictable humorist, who writes as though he were going gently mad."[19]

In the 1930s Bemelmans also began working in the theater, laying the groundwork for the stage and film projects of the 1940s. Early in 1935, shortly after the appearance of *Hansi,* he supervised the preparation of costumes, animals, and scenery for the New York adaptation of *Noah* by French playwright André Obey. In 1938 he rehearsed the small role of a German general in an anti-war play by Nathanael West with Joseph Schrank, *Good Hunting: A Satire in Three Acts.*[20] According to Bemelmans's humorous account in *Town and Country* (and within the month, in *Small Beer*), he was replaced just before opening night.[21] The play itself closed after only two performances; perhaps, as scholar Jay Martin suggests, a delayed opening brought it before the public at a time when developments in Europe had unexpectedly created a pro-war climate in the New York opening-night audience.[22]

The 1940s: New Creative Outlets

Despite his meteoric rise to fame in children's literature in the 1930s, Bemelmans contributed little to the field in the next decade. Appearing first in *Town and Country,* his second Simon & Schuster juvenile, *Fifi* (1940), attempted to use some elements of the *Madeline* formula, with a French poodle as heroine. Two years later both *Town and Country* and Random House printed the fablelike *Rosebud* (called "Nosegay" in the magazine version). In 1947 CBS published *A Tale of Two Glimps,* a witty piece of puffery in praise of color television. Finally, in the December 1949 issue of *Good Housekeeping,* Bemelmans presented "Sunshine Sunshine Go Away," the magazine version of his award-winning book, *Sunshine: A Story about the City of New York,* which Simon & Schuster published the next year.

Bemelmans's relative inactivity in juvenile literature during the 1940s is explained in part by his prodigious creativity in other areas. In 1943 he went to Hollywood to work on the film *Yolanda and the Thief* for MGM. Based on a story he co-authored with Jacques Thery, the 1945 release featured Fred Astaire and Lucille Bremer and was directed by Vincente Minnelli. Bemelmans also began writing novels, presenting them first in magazines before publishing them in hardcover, and thus maintaining a continuous public image. His first, *Now I Lay Me Down to Sleep* (1944), is a satirical and fantastic recounting of the travels of a wealthy Ecuadorian general and his entourage. (In 1950 the work was adapted into a play that Hume Cronyn directed first at Stanford University and then for an eight-week Broadway run. In his autobiographical *A Terrible Liar: A Memoir,* Cronyn writes that "Bemmy" sent humorous letters from all over Europe expressing confidence and support, urging him not to worry too much about it.[23])

Bemelmans's second novel, *The Blue Danube* (1945), pits the good and simple folk of his German hometown, Regensburg, against the hostile

Nazis. The third, *Dirty Eddie* (1947), reveals the zany, profligate, and sometimes lonely Hollywood scene. In his fourth novel, *The Eye of God* (1949), the narrator assumes an Olympian perspective in re-creating the many facets of life in a Tyrolean village during and after World War II.

Bemelmans continued in the 1940s to achieve fame as the author of illustrated books on hotels and travel, often anthologizing them from his magazine articles. An exception to this was *At Your Service: The Way of Life in a Hotel* (1941), a straightforward, factual presentation of hotel-keeping. The humorous *Hotel Splendide* (1941) is based on characters and activities of a New York Hotel that Bemelmans identifies elsewhere as the Ritz-Carlton ("Old Ritz," 157). *The Donkey Inside* (1941) reflects in a variety of moods on visits to South America. A larger format book, *The Best of Times: An Account of Europe Revisited* (1948), contains sadly ironic commentary on a postwar Europe while affording Bemelmans the space he needed for his sophisticated expressionistic paintings. A book of short sketches entitled *I Love You, I Love You, I Love You* (1942) and the anthology *Hotel Bemelmans* (1946)—a reissuing of *Life Class* and *Hotel Splendide* with additional material—complete the work of a decade that saw the publishing of 13 books, a screenplay, and numerous articles.

The Last 12 Years: The Outpouring Continues

In the 1950s and early 1960s Bemelmans returned to children's litera-ture with renewed energy. In 1954 he won the Caldecott for *Madeline's Rescue* and began immediately to capitalize on Madeline's popularity by producing other adventures: *Madeline's Christmas in Texas* (1955, for Neiman Marcus), "Madeline's Christmas" (*McCall's*, 1956), *Madeline and the Bad Hat* (1957), *Madeline and the Gypsies* (1959), and *Madeline in London* (1961). He also produced six other juveniles: *Sunshine: A Story about the City of New York* (1950), *The Happy Place* (1952), *The High World* (1954), *Parsley* (1955), *Welcome Home!* (1960), and *Marina* (1962).

Although Bemelmans was exhibiting his paintings in galleries from at least as early as the 1930s,[24] in *My Life in Art* (1958), he recounts that beginning in 1953 he turned to painting more seriously than before ("Swan Country," 23–24).[25] He showed his works—often scenes from his travels—in a number of places, among them the Hammer Galleries in New York City. In addition to other kinds of paintings, Bemelmans often sold the originals of his children's book illustrations at these gallery exhibits, a practice that increased both revenue and renown. One Hammer brochure for an exhibition of *Parsley* illustrations and landscapes includes a

34-item "Partial List of Bemelmans Collectors," clearly suggesting his popularity among the rich and famous such as Charles Boyer, Joseph Cotton, Alfred Hitchcock, Olivia de Havilland, Helen Hayes, the President of Ecuador, and Aristotle Onassis. The list also reveals that among the purchasers of Bemelmans's works were major museums such as the Metropolitan Museum of Art in New York and the Musée National d'Art Moderne in Paris.[26]

In October 1959 an exhibition of New York scenes opened at the Museum of the City of New York before traveling around the country. Typically, Bemelmans capitalized on this project with the presentation of a number of these works in a dramatic full-color *Holiday* spread the same month.[27]

In the last 12 years of his life, Bemelmans continued to enchant adult readers with sketches and novels. Among the best-known and most often quoted of his humorous, part-fact/part-fiction works is *Father, Dear Father* (1953), which was based on a trip to Europe in the company of his daughter, Barbara. His last such work, *On Board Noah's Ark* (1962), revels in the trials and delights of yachting on the Mediterranean. His biographical tribute to Lady Elsie Mendl, *To the One I Love the Best*, appeared in 1955. Between 1957 and his death, he also published three more novels. In *The Woman of My Life* (1957) he turned for the first time to first-person narration with the memoirs of Armand, an idealistic Parisian duke. In his 1960 work *Are You Hungry Are You Cold,* a teenage French heroine tells of an affectionless childhood with her militarist father and of her consequent retaliation. The posthumous *The Street Where the Heart Lies* (1963) recounts the triumph of love when Parisian *stripeuse* Gala of the Relaxez-Vous nightclub weds a young American *clochard.*

After a year of suffering a number of illnesses, Bemelmans died in his sleep on 1 October 1962. He was buried at Arlington Cemetery. Not long before his death he had closed a letter with the request, "One more thing—I would like to have on my tombstone, 'Tell Them It Was Wonderful'" (M. Bemelmans, xix). Used as the title of his 1985 anthology, the words sum up Bemelmans's exuberant embrace of life's richness and variety.

Bemelmans's Personality and Work Habits

In an article May Massee wrote in 1954 just after Bemelmans had received the Caldecott for *Madeline's Rescue,* she remembered her first impressions of him. He was "genial, witty, shy, and also, as was to be learned, diabolically clever" (Massee, 484) Then in his early thirties, this young artist was likely to write and draw almost anywhere and at any time. In waiting for "the good hour . . . when writing seems effortless and right" he wrote *Hansi* on whatever was at hand: "stubs borrowed from waiters, on the backs of envelopes, old menus, the inside cover of paper matches, and on wrapping paper" ("May Massee," 231). One portion of the original dummy of *Hansi* was made in a restaurant in Munich in 1932 and bound with a toothpick.[28] In 1937 *Newsweek* printed a photo of him in his bathtub, sketching on a board suspended across the top, his typewriter and a glass of wine nearby ("Illustrator," 21).

Bemelmans's energy and drive were phenomenal. *Current Biography 1941* noted that he slept only three or four hours a night and composed mentally while lying awake.[29] This drive stayed with him: years later, in 1954, Massee wrote, "His restless energy can never let him alone—he has so many skills that he is driven from one to another and in between he writes a play or opens a restaurant or takes a Mediterranean cruise—it's all the same to Ludwig."[30] Even when Bemelmans did not appear to be working, one part of his mind was busy: *Time* reported in 1952 that in describing his painting process, he noted, "'I think pleasantly about a picture for a week sometimes, and then do it on the afternoon of the seventh day.'"[31]

Another side of this complex artist was the socially skillful and genial individual. Writing about a 1952 Houston art exhibit, *Time* pictured Bemelmans in a tuxedo smoking a cigar and described his appearance as that of a "happy, well-fed burgomaster" ("People Watcher," 74). Norman Cousins recalls him as the ebullient center of attention at the *Saturday Review*'s weekly get togethers: "Bemelmans was the least inarticulate and most delightful personality I ever encountered."[32]

The cheer that extended outward socially seemed to stem from a genuine goodwill for others. Henry C. Pitz noted that Bemelmans's "optimism and humor" were not "fragile growths." Rather, having survived the destruction of much that was dear to him, these qualities stemmed from an "indestructible faith in the race of humans" (Pitz, 49). In *Father, Dear Father* Bemelmans relays his daughter Barbara's observation that even his bad characters aren't very bad—"they're just odd." To this Bemelmans replies that he finds it "hard to hate anybody, and impossible to hate anybody for long."[33] In a self-portrait he wrote for Donald and Eleanor Friede in his later years, Bemelmans mentions a "cloak of arrogance" that he assumes in order to hide the fact that he is "overly kind, overly generous."[34]

Bemelmans and Houses

Bemelmans seemed always to have enjoyed molding whatever space he occupied to reflect his personality. May Massee describes the Eighth Street Studio, the room in which she first met him, as being "a room with character and imagination and a zest for living" (Massee, 484). Bemelmans had decorated the walls with a cheerful assortment of furniture and objects, including painted cupboards and chests, a cuckoo clock, and a guitar. As his fame increased, so did his means. In the early 1940s the Gramercy Park apartment where he lived with Madeleine and Barbara was filled with the kinds of things he had once only been able to imagine. These eclectic objects—some of them findings from his travels—included a mirror from Quito, a Bavarian chest, a real bird cage, and an impressive French horn. *House and Garden* noted that "the general impression of these rooms . . . is half castle, half peasant cottage."[35]

Bemelmans extended his practice of decorating his homes to public places as well. The scenes he painted on the walls of the Hapsburg House, a Viennese restaurant in New York City of which he was part owner in the early 1930s, were still there at the time of his death.[36] He also decorated a chamber in the Postgasthof, the inn in the Austrian village of Lech am Arlberg that he uses as a setting of *The High World*. In 1947, while living at the Hotel Carlyle with his family, he painted humorous depictions of Parisian street life on the walls of what is known today as the Bemelmans Bar. In a *New York Times* obituary, an unidentified friend stated that Bemelmans's earnings from painting café interiors was at least equal to what he earned from his books.[37]

Bemelmans had a number of dwellings scattered around Europe and in America. For instance, according to Henry C. Pitz, early in the 1950s, Bemelmans had apartments in Paris and Porto D'Ischia, Italy, as well as one in New York. Pitz also noted that Bemelmans owned and managed two inns, a practice that came naturally to a descendent of innkeepers and one that permitted him not only a place to stay during his travels but also the comfort of entertaining luxuriously. Pitz concluded, "He finds it easier to travel to Paris than to Philadelphia. He need not pause to pack a bag even" (Pitz, 48). Late in life Bemelmans's love for boats developed into a full-scale passion for yachting, a lifestyle that permitted him to combine both the comforts of home and the pleasures of a constantly changing scene.

Many of Bemelmans's children's books reflect the sense of security that he assigned to houses. The endpapers of his first, *Hansi,* present a large-scale schematic cutaway of each room of Uncle Herman's Tyrolean dwelling, snuggled deep in the snow. Bemelmans names his next three works after the structures in which they primarily take place: *The Golden Basket*, a hotel in Bruges; *The Castle Number Nine* (1937), a castle with this fanciful address; and *Quito Express* (1938), a train that is baby Pedro's moving home until he returns to his family. Probably one of the most famous houses in children's literature is the "old house in Paris" that harbors Madeline and her friends.[38] *Sunshine: A Story about the City of New York* (1950) deals with a New York housing shortage, and *The High World* (1954) concerns the threats to the home of a Tyrolean mountaineer. *Welcome Home!* (1960), after a poem by Beverley Bogert, delights in the return of clever daddy fox to his cozy hut, where a loving wife and children pamper him after the annual hunt.

The Development of the Author/Artist

Bemelmans seems always to have preferred painting to writing; as he told his daughter Barbara, in *Father, Dear Father* (1953), "I would rather paint than write, for writing is labor" (160). Perhaps fancifully, Bemelmans related to the audience of *Young Wings,* the publication of the Junior Literary Guild, that even as a child in Gmunden he drew pictures with pencil stubs that the maître d' of his father's hotel brought out to him in the garden ("Monsieur Carnewal and the Start of the Story").[39] In "Lausbub" Bemelmans notes that in his youth his Uncle Hans discouraged him in no uncertain terms from becoming an artist "like my father," but that his Aunt gave him watercolors for his birthday (*Tell Them,* 25). Sometime during the first two years that he emigrated to America, he studied to a limited extent in Greenwich Village with someone whom he identifies as "Thaddeus." Bemelmans has written that although this experience taught him "to see," he felt paralyzed as soon as he began to draw. Thaddeus reassured him that confidence would come in time, but only through a process of self-discovery: "'The colors, the design, the line, are all your own, you yourself must get them out.'"[40]

Not only as artist, but also as author, Bemelmans seems to have developed without formal training. His early leave-taking of academia suggests limited instruction in any kind of composition or creative writing. Ethel Heins reports that although Austrian, Bemelmans spoke only French in his early childhood, this being the language of fashion and the language he spoke most "spontaneously" in his adult life.[41] German was acquired next, after moving to Regensburg at the age of six, and English after he came to America. When his daughter, Barbara, asked him whether he thought in German or English, he replied that he thought not in words, but in images: "I see everything in pictures, and then translate them into English. . . . When I write, a man comes in the door. I see it as a movie—I see the door, precisely a certain kind of door, and I see the man (*Father,* 159).

In 1954 he assured the audience at the Caldecott Medal presentation, "I have repeatedly said two things that no one takes seriously, and they are that first of all I am not a writer but a painter, and secondly that I have no imagination."[42] Nine years earlier he had described his story-writing process in words that give some insight into both statements:

> This operation, writing, is always a dreadful, tiresome business and the worst of all tortures for me, because I am convinced that I am not a writer but a graphic workman, a painter who hangs pictures in a row, who collects imagery; and my problem is always to find one for a beginning and one for an end and then, something to hang in the middle so that it resembles a book.[43]

In calling himself "a painter who hangs pictures in a row, a collector of images," Bemelmans suggests his natural inclination for a comic strip form of communication—or for a type of picturebook relying at least as heavily on pictures as on text. In his Caldecott acceptance speech for *Madeline's Rescue,* he noted that he had achieved this in *Madeline:* "There is very little text and there is a lot of picture. The text allows me the most varied type of illustration: there is the use of flowers, of the night, of all of Paris, and such varied detail as the cemetery of Père La Chaise and the Restaurant of the Deux Magots" ("Acceptance," 256).

Throughout the *Madeline* series the image plays a role of equal importance to the text, to some extent determining the story line. For instance, each of the *Madeline* stories had to be built around a reason for moving Madeline through the terrain that Bemelmans desired to depict; this itself suggests actions such as searching for a lost dog, being kidnapped by gypsies, or dashing around town on a runaway horse. Furthermore, Bemelmans composed the stories in terms of images that would appeal to children: food, bed, trains, planes, the sun, uniforms, animals, and other children.

One of Bemelmans's special gifts as "collector of images" was an extraordinary visual memory, both for color and for pattern. His account of a childhood incident in which a teacher slipped on the ice, knocking out his teeth, suggests a remarkable clarity of image recall: "I can see the snow now, and the stain—its exact color—still after more than fifty years, and the house in back of the chain, a mustard-colored Baroque building."[44] He also remembers being deeply affected by color at an even younger age: "Then I was a baby in my carriage. As I was wheeled around the lake every day, I watched its rich emerald green water, the dark pine forests on the slopes of the mountains, the peasant houses in the wide fields. I loved the colors and reached out for them. I also remember the transparent red of a toy balloon I let go as it sailed over the lake and was lost high up, too small to be seen" ("Monsieur Carnewal," 86).

In the Caldecott acceptance speech, as Bemelmans discusses the creation of *Madeline* and then *Madeline's Rescue,* his assertion that he has "no imagination" refers to two separate aspects of his creativity. On the one hand, he refers to the fact that he prefers to create from life—from actual settings, incidents, and characters—rather than from imagination. In the speech he identifies many such ingredients in his own background that have made their way into *Madeline:* his mother's and his own boarding school experiences, a little girl who stood up in the hospital bed next to his and showed an appendix scar, a crack on the hospital ceiling, and a dog pulling something from the Seine. In his view the proximity of his work to real-life gives it vitality: "The portrait of life is the most important work of the artist and it is good only when you've seen it, when you've touched it, when you know it. Then you can breathe life onto canvas and paper" ("Acceptance," 259). As he talks about the upcoming third book in the series, he reveals that he is engaged in looking for the right model for Pepito: "I've been to Spain three times and searched for him and for his house. . . . [S]omewhere he is, lives and breathes." In the same spirit of respect for life's richness, six years later he would instruct an assistant collecting sketches for the horse in *Madeline in London* to "get busy with that horse society . . . [s]ince in life you will always find that which you'd like to imagine and can't."[45]

When Bemelmans says that he has "no imagination," however, he means not only that he prefers to find his inspiration in real-life models; he is referring also to his difficulties in inventing a plot for *Madeline's Rescue,* "for I was paralyzed with lack of imagination" ("Acceptance," 258). To solve his problem, in this instance, he paid the daughters of poet Phyllis McGinley for their suggestion that a dog gets lost and comes back with puppies for everyone. In his other works for children, difficulties in constructing a unifying plot are also apparent. Many are episodic, such as *Hansi* and *The Golden Basket,* which are organized around travel themes. Likewise, the *Madeline* books move from one crisis to the next before the girls return safely home. In a number of his books—*Quito Express*, the *Madeline* books, *Fifi*, and *Marina*—Bemelmans uses the same basic action: a child or other helpless creature gets into trouble and has to be rescued. In other works—*The Castle Number Nine, Madeline's Rescue, The High World*, and *Parsley*—Bemelmans borrows substantial parts of his plots from other sources.

In describing his difficulties as writer, Bemelmans had noted that "my problem is always to find one [image] for a beginning and one for an end, and then something to hang in the middle so that it resembles a book" ("Art for Art's Sake," 55). The formulaic approach of the *Madeline* series, with a relatively constant opening, closing, and repeated phrases and images from book to book, would thus be a natural way for Bemelmans to proceed. Fortunately, such an approach offers a child reader a comfortable sense of familiarity with the story's narrative structure.

In his children's books Bemelmans displays a command of a variety of media, including watercolor, pen and ink, gouache, and conte crayon. As a caricaturist he was extraordinary in his ability to capture with only a line or two the essence of an expression or a movement. His best scenes are full of energy and humor and a vibrant and personal use of color. As a writer of prose, Bemelmans's strengths are his comic pacing, his use of sensory imagery, and his choice of details. On the other hand, his verse wavers between quixotically imperfect and uncomfortably ragged. His adult novels, although enlivened by his never-flagging sense of the incongruous, have many flaws. In the earliest, sudden shifts of perspective and lack of structural proportion jar the reader. In some, excessively long descriptive passages pall. Bemelmans was clearly at his best when he could simultaneously communicate through pictures and words, in a medium where the sustained verbal development of character, setting, and action was unnecessary. He thus found his natural milieu in his children's picturebooks and in his illustrated verbal sketches for adults.

Children's Books

Bemelmans's children's books share many similarities with his adult literature. Inasmuch as most of his adult literature is illustrated, albeit to a lesser extent than his works for children, both are forms of storytelling in which words and pictures work together. In mood, they are humorous, often ironic, and occasionally satiric. As is usually the case with humor, characters are types rather than fully developed individuals. In 1953 critic Lee Rogow also noted similarities of subject matter and values: both his adult works and those for children typically involve traveling and attention to food and drink. Children, old ladies, and other humble creatures are valued and ultimately protected. His villains "are the petty officials who misuse power to trample on the rights of the good people and the good dogs" (Rogow, 13).

During his lifetime Bemelmans wrote and illustrated 19 books for children. He also created a Neiman Marcus giveaway entitled *Madeline's Christmas in Texas* and a magazine book insert, *Madeline's Christmas,* which was published in a different format in 1985. Additionally, he illustrated *Noodle* by Munro Leaf. His books for juvenile readers may conveniently be discussed in three categories: those leading up to *Madeline,* *Madeline* and the sequels, and the post-*Madeline* books.

As one might expect, given the similarities between his works for children and those for adults, many of the former also appealed to older readers. In fact, a notable aspect of the reviews of his books for children was the frequency with which this point was made. In his earliest books, those written for May Massee, this seems to have been a fortunate but unintended result. With *Madeline,* however, Bemelmans's picturebooks begin to change. No longer do they seem "incidentally" to appeal to adults; instead, they seem intentionally targeted to adults, at least as much as, and in many cases more than, to children. Bemelmans himself said, "I never in my life wrote for children. I write for myself" ("Madeline's Master," 115). Although an exaggeration, the comment contains a good deal of truth.

Beginning with *Madeline,* like much else that he wrote, Bemelmans presented nearly all of his children's books in adult magazines. He noted in a letter to Massee that such a practice increased his revenues and benefited the publisher in terms of free printing plates and free advertising.[46] Some of these works were more clearly intended for a dual readership than others. For instance, those that appeared in "family" magazines such as *McCall's* were offerings that either the adult or the youngster might read to himself, or that parents and children might share. On the other hand, it seems more likely that Bemelmans's first audience for works like *Fifi* or *Nosegay* (later called *Rosebud*), which appeared first in the sophisticated *Town and Country,* consisted primarily of adults.

Especially noteworthy is the number of times that Bemelmans's "children's" books first appeared in Christmas issues. The first such December offering, "Sunshine, Sunshine Go Away," ends with the

Scrooge-like landlord returning at Christmas to be reconciled with the music-making tenant. A full-color picture shows Miss Moore leading carols around a decorated tree in Gramercy Park.[47] The second story, "Christmas in Tyrol," tells a story that stretches from one Christmas to another, concluding with a special recipe for "Tyrolean glow-wine."[48] Although Christmas does not figure into the setting of "Madeline's Rescue," the story was obviously meant to evoke the childhood joys of the season when the work first appeared in the December 1951 *Good Housekeeping,* described as "Our Best and Happiest Christmas Issue." Madeline's association with Christmas was further heightened when the next two *Madeline* stories to appear in magazines both were called "Madeline's Christmas." The first work so titled, appearing in the December 1955 *Good Housekeeping,* was published the same year as a book with the title *Madeline's Christmas in Texas;* the second, a December 1956 *McCall's* book insert, was published by Viking in 1985 as *Madeline's Christmas.* What emerges from this list is an image of Bemelmans as a jolly Santa Claus whose stories made the magazine a Christmas gift from the publisher to the reader. In fact, the December 1958 *McCall's* book insert, *Madeline and the Gypsies,* bears the inscription "A *McCall's* Christmas gift for the whole family."

Under the tutelage of Viking's influential May Massee, Bemelmans molded his first four works to accepted norms of juvenile publishing. *Hansi, The Golden Basket,* and *Quito Express* focus on the experiences of one or more child protagonists exploring foreign lands. All express wholesome values and communicate a sense of security. The first two, in particular, correspond to the Massee preference for a dependence on the text and a high standard of fairly representational art. Even the least conventional of the early works, *The Castle Number Nine,* uses a traditional fairy-tale setting and concludes with a moral.

Certainly *Madeline* subscribes to many of the above conventions, yet in other ways it forges new approaches to works for juvenile readers, approaches that initially seemed aimed at an adult readership. The book's illustrations—cartoons and expressionistic watercolors—the heavy dependence on pictures to communicate much of the information, and the ironic conclusion all suggest that Bemelmans expected to please adults as well as children. This dual readership worked to ensure the book's popularity, and Bemelmans responded with sequels following the same formulae, eventually creating a classic series.

Aside from the sequels, Bemelmans was never again as successful in addressing both audiences at once as he was in *Madeline.* In fact, in one way or another, the post-*Madeline* books display a certain disregard for the young reader. First of all, most lack a child protagonist; Marina, a baby seal, provides the only exception. Furthermore, in direct violation of children's literature's long-revered goal to mold young minds and spirits, in some of these books, Bemelmans seems unconcerned about the value of the lesson he imparts. In others, the experiences, language, and sources of humor seem more appropriate for adults than for children.

"Count Bric a Brac": A Comic Strip for All Ages

Among Bemelmans's earliest extant published works is a comic strip called "Thrilling Adventures of Count Bric a Brac." According to bibliographer Murray Pomerance, the work first appeared in the *New York World* on 4 July 1926 and ran on Sundays "at least" through 7 January 1927 (Pomerance, 266–67). Bill Blackbeard, director of the San Francisco Academy of Comic Arts, has also located the work in the *Milwaukee Journal* on Sundays during the fall of 1926. The strip provides an insight into Bemelmans's beginnings as "graphic workman" ("Art for Art's Sake," 55).

In "The Old Ritz" Bemelmans reveals that for many years while working in hotel restaurants to earn a living, his avowed ambition was to be a newspaper cartoonist. Standing behind a palm tree, in idle moments he would sketch clients on the backs of menus. Finally, he writes, "by 1926, after years of work and countless disappointments, it seemed as if I had achieved my goal. I sat up in the cupola of the old *World* building with a group of funnymen: Webster, Milt Gross, Ernie Bushmiller, and Haenigsen. Walter Berndt, who drew 'Smitty' in the *Daily News,* helped me a great deal. There was constant laughter in that cupola" ("Old Ritz," 158).

The variety of publications in which "Count Bric a Brac" appeared suggests that from the very beginning Bemelmans's work was considered appropriate for both adults and children. According to Bill Blackbeard, the "witty and sophisticated" work was used as "adult relief" in the *World*'s magazine section (telephone interview, 6 August 1991). Yet copies of the strip from the *Milwaukee Journal* from September through December 1926 suggest that one newspaper, at least, placed it in the children's section (and always on page 7). The articles on the backs of these pages include a selection from Hugh Lofting's *Dr. Doolittle,* a story about fairies, nature features by Thornton Burgess, and teenage club news (*Milwaukee Journal,* 1926).

"Thrilling Adventures of Count Bric a Brac" provides evidence that early in his career Bemelmans used techniques common to cartoonists that he would also use later in his more successful children's books. One of his sources of inspiration may have been German poet, cartoonist, and artist Wilhelm Busch, for whose humor, according to Madeleine Bemelmans, he "had a great appreciation."[49] A comparison of "Count Bric a Brac" and Busch's most famous work, *Max und Moritz, Eine Bubengeschichte in sieben Streichen* (1865; *Max and Moritz, a Boys' Story in Seven Pranks*), shows that even in his earliest visual storytelling, Bemelmans's work had similarities to that of this German master.

One of the techniques essential to the comic strip artist is the creation of a standardized representation of a character, a uniquely identifying image that can be "read" quickly. Will Eisner, creator of the comic strip "The Spirit," explains in *Comics and Sequential Art* that the comic strip artist expects his reader to "read" images with much the same ease that he reads words; the pictures function as part of a total narrative effort to communicate efficiently.[50] Busch's Max and Moritz, for instance, are distinguished by their markedly different hairstyles. Similarly, Bemelmans's reader can identify Count Bric a Brac by his long pointy noise; his friend, the Professor, is recognizable by his full white beard. Later, in the *Madeline* series, Bemelmans would provide quickly identifiable, consistent outlines for principal characters: Breton roller hats, hairbows, and capes for Madeline and her friends; a nun's robes and headpiece for Miss Clavel; and a cape and a tall hat with pom-poms for Pepito.

Wilhelm Busch narrated *Max and Moritz* as well as other picture stories in rhymed couplets, a practice that, according to Maurice Horn, influenced German picture-stories up through the 1930s.[51] Max and Moritz, the acknowledged predecessors of the Katzenjammer Kids, devise ingenious torments for each of their stuffy neighbors in turn. Finally, the boys meet an outrageous fate when Farmer Klein has the Miller grind them into bits:

> Rickle-rackle, rickle-rackle,
> Hear the millstones grind and crackle.
> Here is what the mill releases:
> Still themselves, but all in pieces.
> And the miller's ducks are there
> To devour the loose-knit pair.[52]

One of the more obvious links between Bemelmans and Busch, whose works he doubtless read in the original, lies in the continuance of this tradition. In the "Thrilling Adventures of Count Bric a Brac," Bemelmans sometimes, although not always, placed verse in the mouth of his protagonist. *Newsweek* for 24 July 1937 relates Bemelmans's pleasure in recalling such "gems" as "What comes there far away and distant? / Must be the plumber and his assistant" (21). In fact, says *Newsweek,* such poetry contributed to Bemelmans's being "peremptorily fired from his $50-a-week job": "*World* readers failed to appreciate his subtlety. They didn't like the Count or the poetry he recited." Bemelmans later used rhymed couplets to narrate the *Madeline* books, *Fifi, Sunshine,* and *Marina,* as well as the original magazine version of *Rosebud,* entitled "Nosegay."

In *Max and Moritz* Busch satirizes the objects of his hellion's torments through their ridiculous portraiture and the fates that befall them.[53] Similarly, Bemelmans introduces satire into "The Thrilling Adventures of Count Bric a Brac." Although the Count often gets the upper hand in a sticky situation, sometimes the entire strip culminates in a low-key joke based on flaws such as his tight-fistedness, gluttony, or laziness. In a strip in the *Milwaukee Journal* for 12 December 1926, Bemelmans takes a jab at European aristocracy when the Count tells the Professor, "As a count I am expert at NOT working" (7). Bemelmans also amuses his *Journal* readers with mild mockery of other subjects: the woman blabbermouth and Mexican revolutionaries (28 November 1926, 7), as well as Russian "comrades" (12 December 1926, 7). Later Bemelmans would lace many of his children's works with touches of satire. In fact, the timorous elderly female travelers of *The Golden Basket* who are scared by knight's armor that suddenly seems to come to life are preceded by a similar pair in "Count Bric a Brac" for the *Milwaukee Journal,* 14 November 1926. Among the many other caricatures of Bemelmans's children's books are the overly precise Baptiste in *The Castle Number Nine,* the miserly Sunshine and the naive Miss Moore in *Sunshine: A Story about the City of New York,* the heartless trustees in *Madeline's Rescue,* and the pompous Herr Oberministerialrat in *The High World.*

As early as "Count Bric a Brac" Bemelmans displayed the visual sophistication that was to distinguish the best of his children's books to come. Noting Bemelmans's creative use of layout, Blackbeard calls the strip "a graphic knockout" (telephone interview, 6 August 1991). Across the top of each series stretches a panorama that establishes the setting, a device that anticipates the endpapers of his picturebooks. Bemelmans divides up his page in frames of whatever sizes best fit his visual needs, rather than dividing the space into even squares. An early example of Bemelmans's personal use of color is the consistent use of a black sky even in daytime scenes, a technique that lends a somewhat dreamlike atmosphere to the proceedings.

Even as early as "The Thrilling Adventures of Count Bric a Brac" Bemelmans pursued the theme of travel. From week to week, the smiling Count visited different tourist attractions, often accompanied by the Professor. The Count, who appears to be in his twenties or thirties, wears the native garb, appearing in such costumes as lederhosen or Russian furs. Clearly, the strip intends to inform while entertaining: a placard at the outset gives a fact or two about the setting, and the frames reveal detail in the portrayal of foreign architecture and scenery.

The professional traveler was to become one of Bemelmans's best-known personas in his literature for adults. Foreign settings provide the backdrop for a majority of his children's books as well. What emerges from such diverse placement of "Count Bric a Brac" as the magazine section of the *World* and a childen's section of the *Milwaukee Journal* is the sense that from the beginning of his career, Bemelmans's appeal transcended neat limitations of age. At its worst, this quality lent itself to the production of books of slight merit for anyone. At its best, it contributed to the creation of a classic series.

Chapter Two

Children's Books for Children: The Massee Influence

Bemelmans served his apprenticeship in children's literature under the influential May Massee of Viking Press. Consequently, *Hansi, The Golden Basket, The Castle Number Nine,* and *Quito Express* all reflect norms prevalent in the world of juvenile publishing in the late 1930s. The fact that *Hansi, The Golden Basket,* and *Quito Express* all dealt humorously, factually, and in a graphically appealing manner with foreign travel made them highly appealing to adults as well. Although the first two books contain many illustrations, they depend most heavily upon their texts to convey information. *The Castle Number Nine,* however, represents a form of storytelling in which words and pictures are more nearly equally important, an evolution that foreshadowed *Madeline.* In the same year that Viking published *The Castle Number Nine,* Bemelmans did the illustrations for Munro Leaf's *Noodle,* published by F. A. Stokes. This project showed him the possibility of expanding his market while doing a somewhat less demanding kind of book, thus making his profession more financially secure.

Hansi

As she did with many other talented authors and artists, Viking editor May Massee "discovered" Ludwig Bemelmans. In a 1936 *Hornbook* section devoted to an appreciation of Massee's contributions to children's literature, Bemelmans wrote,

About seven years ago a typographer brought Miss Massee to my house for dinner. It was a dreary building of six rooms in a noisy neighborhood. The windows of my living room looked out at a cobweb of telegraph wires, a water tank, and a Claude Neon sign that flashed "Two Pants Suits at $15.00." To hide this *mise en scene,* and because I was homesick for my mountains, I had painted outside of my windows a field with blue gentians, the foothills around Innsbruck, and a peasant house with a Forester sitting in front of it, on his lap a wire-haired dachshund, and a long pipe dividing his white beard. "You must write children's books," decided Miss Massee. ("May Massee," 231)

Hansi, published in 1934, was the result of this encouragement and collaboration. It was not only Bemelmans's first children's book but also his first published book of any kind. The pictures in his living room all find their way into it: Innsbruck is Hansi's home city; Uncle Herman's house is there, and so is the dachshund, now named Waldl. *Hansi*'s circular, episodic plot describes Hansi's journey to relatives in the Tyrol and back home again to his mother. No sooner has the Christmas vacation begun than Hansi finds himself on a train puffing high into the mountains. An exciting adventure occurs when he and his cousin Lieserl strap skis to Waldl, and the dachshund sails off down the mountain, becoming lost for much of the day. The story culminates in the celebration of Christmas Eve, with the Three Kings singing from door to door and a late-night service in the village church. In the last chapter Hansi returns to his mother, bringing his new mountaineering clothes and the hope of a return visit the following summer.

From cartoonist to picturebook artist/author.   Bemelmans's first efforts at visual storytelling had been in the form of the comic strip "Thrilling Adventures of Count Bric a Brac" (1926). In the 1930s he continued to produce cartoons for adult magazines, including the wordless "Noodles, the Trained Seal" for the *Saturday Evening Post* in 1933, "The Count and the Cobbler" in *Harper's Bazaar* in 1935, and two wordless cartoons in *Town and Country* in 1939.[1] For two years beginning 8 March 1935, he produced a weekly series about a trained seal named "Silly Willy" for the readers of *Young America* (Pomerance, 267). As he was to observe in 1945, he more readily considered himself to be a "graphic workman, a painter who hangs pictures in a row" than a writer ("Art for Art's Sake," 55). Thus *Hansi,* a work in which the greatest weight of the narration is borne by a full text, and in which the many illustrations reveal a more sensitive and realistic style than Bemelmans's cartoons, represents a new authorial direction. A comparison of the early stages of *Hansi* with the final product shows that Bemelmans left the elements of comic strip storytelling behind as he moved closer to the book. A letter he wrote to Massee during this process suggests that his desire to conform to her standards was what led him to make these changes.

The first partial dummy for *Hansi,* dated 1932, bears very little resemblance to the final work. This document, donated by Bemelmans to the New York Public Library, bears the inscription "Part of the first dummy for 'Hansi' made in Munich 1932 and bound with a toothpick (the dummy was made in a Restaurant) L. B."[2] Only the Austrian setting, the presence of boy protagonists, and a character named Uncle Herman find their way into the final product. The plot is primarily a frame for the legend of St. Hubert's Stag: after two boys go fishing in the millpond they go to their Uncle Herman's house, where he tells them of St. Hubert's Stag before they return home to eat the fish. The action is communicated primarily through a series of full-page pictures, with space indicated on each page for text. On the portion dedicated to the legend, the pages are completely blank except for the word "stag." The children's faces have the stereotypical round cheeks and pointy eyebrows of comic strip youngsters.

Another dummy, although undated, would seem to follow sometime after the 1932 "St. Hubert's Stag" version. In this one the story is clearly about a boy whose mother sends him on a train trip, and the proportion of illustrations and text are much closer to those of the final publication.[3]

An undated letter Bemelmans sent to Massee suggests that it was her views on cartooning that guided the changes from the 1932 version to the final product. From a farm in the country where he had retired for a few days to struggle with "cartoonitis," he wrote,

> —From the time I left you last week until today the problem of curing the epidemic [of cartoonitis] has been my chief concern—and worried me— . . . After moping—sitting—walking and laying about for some time—I come to these conclusions—
>
> 1. You are right cartooning is cheap—vaudeville on paper— . . . most certainly there is no room for slapstick in a childrens [sic] book. As to overcoming it—if will has anything to do with it—yes—I want to do nothing so much as this book and for it will go to any end to do it right. . . .
>
> Now I think to secure your ease of mind—before we go on with any definite work—I should like to make so much of pictures—as will prove that the cartoon feel is definitely thrown out.[4]

Continuing, Bemelmans states that he needs to work "where I can see you—show you work from day to day and constantly—because this is my first book have your advise [sic]—and that I can hardly ask—after all you are not running a school for childrens [sic] book makers."

The art style finally achieved in *Hansi* shows a considerable evolution from the comic strip style suggested by the 1932 "St. Hubert's Stag" dummy. Characters' features, although simplified, are sensitive, and despite the fact that figures are stylized, the depth and texture created through shading and color give a sense of realism. The lithographs, for which Bemelmans's friend Kurt Wiese did the separations, have a soft, crayonlike appearance. The childlike quality of the art is underscored by Bemelmans's indication that the first of the drawings is the work of his child protagonist: "Hansi made this picture himself."[5] And although the narrator makes no claim that Hansi drew the rest of the book's pictures, the transition in style is very subtle.

Massee would later describe Bemelmans's intense efforts to get the pictures exactly right, working all day, then discarding and starting over. She expressed delight in the resulting drawings: "full of the spirit of place, color, humor, and life, full of sentiment without a bit of sentimentality, childlike but never cute, with an integrity that belongs to the artist as well as the sturdy people in the book" (Massee, 485).

The many illustrations in *Hansi* amplify the text, establishing setting, character, and tone; nevertheless, the text takes the lead in the storytelling, communicating with words many things that are never pictured. As another of Massee's protégés, Robert McCloskey, observed, "To her the text was the most important part of the book."[6] For immigrant Bemelmans, the lengthy text of *Hansi* must have been a challenge; Massee's editorial assistance was doubtless invaluable. Much of the charm of Bemelmans's slow-paced evocation of the Tyrol comes through his use of sensory imagery, a quality that imbues his later prose as well. In this passage, for instance, he revels in sights, sounds, and smells, imparting calm and delight: "When they [the horses] shook their heads and looked around, the long rows of jingle bells sang. The sun shone through the clear mountain air. From the bakery across the street came the appetizing fragrance of freshly baked bread. There was the smell of hay and of paint on the old sleigh."

Bemelmans was grateful for Massee's assistance and teaching. In a copy of *Hansi* that he presented to her in 1934 not long after its publication, he enclosed his first sketch for the book, a crayon-on-vellum drawing of a train disappearing into a tunnel. In a posture of respectful, shy gratitude, he signed it, "I can just hold my hat in both hands and turn it—and look down on it and say—thank you lady."[7]

Conforming to juvenile norms. *Hansi* did not simply reveal the high quality of art and text expected of children's books in the 1930s but also conformed to other essential norms of juvenile publishing: an emphasis on the experiences of a child protagonist, the discovery of other cultures, and an ambience of security.

As he portrayed his child protagonist, Bemelmans reached back to memories of his own childhood. In terms of situation there are obvious similarities: like Hansi, Bemelmans grew up without a father; and, according to one source, *Hansi*'s plot sprang partly from Bemelmans's memories of a similar journey to visit an uncle Hans in the Tyrolean Alps.[8] More essential, however, is the fact that Bemelmans clearly succeeded in a goal he expressed to Massee in the letter cited earlier: "For the time I work on this book I must put all other work aside [*sic*] go back to my own childhood for simple honest feeling." In *Hansi* he expresses emotions known to any child anywhere—the joy at escaping school for the holidays, the sadness of leaving a parent, and the awe of Christmas Eve. He understands Hansi's inability to say his fine speech to his new relatives when he first meets them and the comfort of a dog in such a situation. He understands, too, that when Uncle Herman announces at dinner that Hansi must now return home, "the goose turned to putty—and the plum cake got stuck in his throat." The sensitive lips and introspective eyes of the child on the cover, peering through a window frame, suggest Bemelmans the child/adult looking back. (The image is somewhat reminiscent of a picture in Ingri and Edgar Parin d'Aulaire's *Ola* [1932], where the young Norwegian boy Ola, with sweet face and dreamy eyes, looks through a snow-covered window.)

As was typical of so many of his works to come, Bemelmans reveals in *Hansi* his own attachment to animals, an attachment shared by many children, lonely or not. Romulus and Schimmele, the Percherons (draft horses), are appealingly portrayed as intelligent, feeling creatures, engaged with their owners in a mutually beneficial relationship. A horse-drawn sleigh journey to put out feed for the snow-bound deer is the adventure of an entire chapter. In another episode Hansi and his cousin, meaning to be kind to the short-legged dachshund Waldl, attach skis to him with comic results.

One of the most obvious ways in which *Hansi* conformed to current trends in juvenile publishing was its foreign setting. Barbara Bader points out that in the 1930s the joyful exploration of other cultures was a vital trend in American picturebook production. Immigrant artists such as Ingri and Edgar Parin d'Aulaire, Françoise (Seignobosc), Maud and Miska Petersham, Boris Artzybasheff, and (second-generation) Wanda Gág introduced to American children the people, customs, geography, folklore, and art styles of Europe and Russia. Travelers Kurt

Wiese, Thomas Handforth, Erick Berry, and Armstrong Sperry evoked the flavors of Asia and Africa.[9] This excitement over the educational and visual possibilities of multicultural picturebooks had no doubt enhanced Massee's confidence in Bemelmans's marketability as she studied the Austrian scenes painted on his studio walls.

To the didactic aim of teaching Tyrolean customs, language, foods, artifacts, and geography, Bemelmans devotes both words and pictures. For instance, in a chapter entitled "About Clouds and *Lebkuchen*," Hansi and the reader learn that clouds can occasionally roll down the streets of the mountaintop villages and that when this happens, one must stay indoors. Stuck in the kitchen, he subsequently learns to make *Lebkuchen,* "the wonderful brown Christmas cakes"—and the text, directing us to the inserted illustrations, reads, "They looked like this." In another instance, when the text describes Post Seppl's "top hat, white buckskin breeches, and high black boots," Bemelmans's illustrations carefully depict the items mentioned.

In both words and pictures Bemelmans reveals his love for the Tyrolean dwellings and their harmony with nature: "Mountain houses are fine and simple because they have grown from the rock on which they stand, from the forests that are around them, and from the work of men who looked at mountains all their lives and to whom every tree and flower said, 'See how lovely we are in delicate colors and strong clean pattern.'"

The book's striking endpapers reveal a cutaway of Uncle Herman's house, with each activity proceeding in an orderly fashion and each object securely in its place. The many details, so intriguing to eye and mind, portend the best of Bemelmans to come. (During World War II, when Viking was unable to get heavy enough stock, Uncle Herman's house was bound into the book on regular pages.[10])

The security of Uncle Herman's home is but one of several ways in which *Hansi* communicates the atmosphere of protectiveness and love so typical of juvenile works of the era. Despite the unexplained absence of his father, Hansi's existence is warm and secure. Tempering the adventure of leaving home are the loving adults at every step of the way, beginning with his mother, who provides him with food, careful instructions, and a final hooking of his coat collar "so no cold air could get in to Hansi." The large, solid-looking stationmaster takes Hansi by the hand, saying "This way, my young friend," as he delivers him to the sleigh-driver, Post Seppl. Once in Uncle Herman's house, Hansi's relatives see to his every need, physical and emotional, surprising him with a com-

From Hansi *(New York: Viking, 1934). Reprinted by permission of International Creative Management, Inc. Copyright © 1962 by Ludwig Bemelmans.*

plete Tyrolean outfit the first morning he awakens in his painted bed. The warmth of blankets, the comfort of food, and the ruggedness of the house itself—there for two centuries—provide a haven all the more wonderful in contrast with the deep snow outside.

The cyclical plot that brings Hansi back to Innsbruck in itself offers the security of a return to mother and home. This narrative structure, long traditional in children's books, is typical of some of the more enduring Viking works of the 1930s and 1940s: Marjorie Flack/Kurt Wiese's *The Story about Ping* (1933); Munro Leaf/Robert Lawson's *The Story of Ferdinand* (1936); and Robert McCloskey's *Blueberries for Sal* (1948).

In writing about *Hansi* Massee stressed that a sense of security in a children's book offers children the time and freedom to enjoy themselves creatively: "The story is full of kindliness, cleanliness, and order as well as other basic virtues that make for good living and give children a chance to play" (Massee, 485). Not only are these qualities implicit in the characterizations, settings, and plot structure of *Hansi:* the "chance to play" that they offer the child is borne out in the many gentle pastimes pursued by Hansi and Lieserl. They examine the fascinating box of family mementos, they explore the barn, and from barrel staves they make skis for Waldl. The reader, too, is drawn into their fun with an invitation to close one's eyes and draw a pig. Bemelmans even shares directions for putting the icing on *Lebkuchen.*

The book was so well liked that it appeared in several different English-language editions between 1934 and 1940; in 1953 there appeared a Japanese edition (Pomerance, 65–66). *New York Times* critic Anne T. Eaton called *Hansi* "a good book for a Christmas gift for 7 to 9 year olds and even for grown-ups who love the Austrian Tyrol."[11] Thus Bemelmans's ability to entice grown-ups with his children's books was noted from the very beginning of his career. Years later the chapter entitled "About Clouds and *Lebkuchen*" was included in Donald and Eleanor Friede's anthology of Bemelmans's writings, *La Bonne Table* (1964), a work marketed to an adult audience.

The Golden Basket

With only his second book, Bemelmans achieved one of the highest accolades afforded in children's book publishing: the 1937 Newbery Honor Award. Just as in *Hansi,* the didactic intent to teach foreign customs and geography controls the narrative of *The Golden Basket.* At the story's outset, two little English girls, Celeste and Melisande, arrive in Bruges, Belgium, with their father, Mr. Coggeshall. At the story's close, they board a ship to return home. In the intervening chapters, they explore the fascinating inner life of a grand old inn named the Golden Basket, as well as Bruges itself.

Creation of the book. *The Golden Basket* was about a year and a half in the making. February 1935 saw the opening of *Noah,* a play for which Bemelmans had prepared costumes, animals, and scenery. Soon he and his bride, Mimi (Madeleine), were aboard a ship to Belgium to collect material for a new children's book. A letter to May Massee dated 12 April 1935 from Bruges, written as he listens to the music of the town's famous old carillon, says that he is taking photographs and has made 250 sketches "of everything, down to doorhandles and up to chimney pots." He notes that he is sending the ending for the book right away and that he wants her to let him know "in the words and gesture of the last act of *Noah*— 'that's fine' . . . you above all must be absolutely satisfied."[12]

The book, however, was not nearly finished. Much remained to be done, and Bemelmans was on his way to Regensburg, Germany, where his "mother has a nice house, a good cook and I have a studio large enough to put forty men or eight horses to bed in, also a drawing table absolute peace of mind and the distance from which I will see what I have seen a little more clearly" (letter of 12 April 1935).

But inspiration eluded him in a Germany under Nazi rule. On 8 May 1935 he again wrote Massee, describing his unhappiness in this overly regimented society, his creative difficulties, and his decision to return to America "to finish this work":

> The beautiful german horse chestnut trees have begun to blossom yester-day at three o'clock, the hour set for this function by the ministry of spring and of public enlightenment. At six in the morning little girls of, I judge about three years of age, marched trough [*sic*] the streets of this city in batallion formation four abreast and sang "eins—zwei—drei—der Mai ist gekommen die Baeume schlagen aus" the wonders of this new Germany never cease. . . .
>
>   To my unruly nature that kind of precision is unbearable—it rules out all chance of surpise [*sic*] or disappointment and I am packing, that is Mimi is packing our trunks to go on board the Rex on the sixteenth of May and sail back.
>
>   I have watched the trees yesterday at three and hoped one of them might refuse to blossom, but they were alight in the best chremnitz white at exactly three to the last candle. . . . [A]ll this would not have driven me away—because it is fascinating—but I cannot get anything done to my own satisfaction.[13]

Bemelmans describes himself writing and rewriting the text, drawing and tearing up pictures: "In my mind the pictures are quite done—the whole book finished, somehow interference appears when I wish to set it on paper." He strongly feels that the book will be better if he can work more closely with Massee: "I have almost what I want, but not quite—I need you very badly because you will know exactly what we can do" (letter of 8 May 1935).

Bemelmans encountered still other difficulties before *The Golden Basket* was completed. According to a newspaper item that appeared when the book came out in September 1936, at some point during his stay in Germany, the authorities seized the manuscript, "presumably fearing it was anti-Nazi propaganda. However, it was returned with the comment that it was a 'very charming story.'" The article also notes that once back in America, Bemelmans finished the work, only to have all the illustrations destroyed in a fire in his Manhattan studio.[14]

The Newbery Honor Award.   The awarding of the 1937 Newbery Honor Award clearly illustrates the book's acceptance by those who established the norms of children's book publishing. Bemelmans shows sensitivity to the small discoveries of children exploring an old inn and a historic city. His choice of details and his pacing are lively. His episodic chapters have action and humor, with the last chapters forming a kind of climax: a long-anticipated boating trip results in a dousing in a canal and in a subsequent farcical adventure in an old museum.

Like *Hansi, The Golden Basket* is an amply illustrated text, rather than a picturebook. The frequent illustrations play a vital role in establishing characters and foreign settings, clarifying key terms, and enhancing particularly dramatic or comic actions. Consisting of black and white sketches and full-color drawings, they vary in size, placement on the page, and framing devices. Barbara Bader points out that the book's unique color tones—"what one connoisseur called 'a fruitiness'"—are the result of preseparated half-tone printing by William Glaser of the Jersey City Printing Company (Bader, 50). Perhaps critics Linda Kauffman Peterson and Marilyn Leathers Solt are correct in suggesting that the illustrations attracted the Newbery at a time when the Caldecott had not yet been established.[15]

Both visually and verbally, *The Golden Basket* reveals Bemelmans's fascination with the way things look. First, unusual perspectives are explored. The front cover and endpapers dramatically depict the city from above. Lying on his back in bed, Jan, the innkeeper's son, looks up through a skylight at clouds, stars, "the shadows of birds," and a large cat who stares back.[16] In two pictures, Bemelmans shows his subjects standing before mirrors, thus drawing them from front and back at the same time. Second, mechanical devices for affecting an image—a lorgnette, a monocle, a camera, and glasses—figure in characterization or storyline. Finally, verbal similes reveal a highly creative visual imagination. For instance, he writes, "The smooth road was lined with trees and the sun cast their shadows across: it seemed like an endless strip of zebra skin" (*GB,* 92). The seagulls that follow the steamer "looked like opened newspapers on strings" (*GB,* 95).

Bemelmans's portrayal of the tiny delights and happy pastimes of Celeste, Melisande, and Jan reveals the same fine sensitivity to a child's perspective that imbues *Hansi.* Two English ladies in the dining room can be told apart by their furs: one fox has crossed eyes. The girls are fascinated by the marvelous contents of M Carnewal's tailcoat pockets, all carefully depicted in an accompanying illustration. Catching live flies for Jan's frog, a wet indoor game of submarine, and an expedition in the boat that Jan built himself afford great pleasure; a tiny flower tenaciously gripping one of the crevices of the carillon elicits a tender kiss.

A particularly exciting moment for any child is waking up in a strange new room, especially one with a cord hanging within reach, light coming from "two pink glass lilies that grew out of the wall" (*GB,* 8), and amazing red wallpaper and furniture. After hopping out of a bed so high they have to jump onto pillows, the girls stand on their balcony and watch the day begin. Here Bemelmans's recent work on *Noah* comes to mind, for both in text and illustrations he depicts this scene as if the girls were in box seats watching the opening act of a play. Typically, Bemelmans entices his reader to examine his illustration carefully, and way over there, in the only window where light is shining, are the silhouettes of Celeste and Melisande. His double-page illustration of the square at night suggests a stage set "painted on the sky" (*GB,* 10). After the carillon bells finish playing, church bells ring, and, as if entering a stage on cue, "two little old ladies in black dresses hurried across the square" (*GB,* 11). The sunlight spreading from one building to the next suggests the drama of the stage lights coming up from black. The pigeons shake themselves awake, and for three more paragraphs various workers of Bruges enter and begin their daily activities.

The Golden Basket provides the ultimate childhood delight—adventure in comfort:

> Through this window the little girls were looking for the first time in their lives into an altogether new world, with a new language, new policemen, pastry shops, and lampposts. Even the horses and dogs and clouds seemed different. Only the sparrows and pigeons looked the same as they did anywhere else.

The children were cold. They closed the window. . . .

Warm air came up the stairs. It brought pleasure for the nose—somebody was cooking coffee and warming rolls; and from somewhere came the sound of scrubbing. (*GB*, 15)

Cushioning the adventures of this "altogether new world," the hotel, like Uncle Herman's house in *Hansi,* acts as a friendly, clean, and ordered center of activities, a point of departure and return. L'Hotel du Panier d'Or, the Golden Basket Inn, seems to the reader a kind of large and many-cabined ship, a protection against the wonderful rain that pours down on Bruges for days as the story begins, forcing indoor activities. Such an imagined transformation brings to mind not only *Noah,* but also the name of Bemelmans's father's hotel in Gmunden, the Golden Ship.

The adults in the book treat the children with respect and tender affection, protecting, tolerating, entertaining, and explaining. The humorous sight of Mr. Coggeshall's overcoat apparently supported by three pairs of legs appears on the opening page; only on the next page does it become apparent that he is sheltering his two tired little daughters beneath that great expanse of cloth (*GB*, 5–6).

Previews of *Madeline*.   A brief vignette in *The Golden Basket* presents a number of elements that bear a striking resemblance to those Bemelmans was to develop more fully in *Madeline.* Celeste, Melisande, and their father, ambling about in Bruges, encounter the promenading students of the Sacred Heart—12 of them walking in pairs with their "lovely, tall, and never severe Madame Severine" (*GB*, 51)—the fictional predecessors of the "twelve little girls in two straight lines"[17] and Miss Clavel. Just as Madeline lives in "an old house in Paris," these students live in a "great square white house" (*GB*, 53) at the edge of the canal. Even more notable than the depiction of 12 little girls out walking in pairs in *The Golden Basket* is the brief introduction of Madeline's prototype—"Madeleine": "The name of the smallest girl is Madeleine. Her hair is copper-red" (*GB*, 51). The "greatest joy" (*GB*, 52) of this innocent charmer as she walks along at the very back of the row next to Madame Severine is to put her white-gloved finger "into the grooves on buildings and slide it along, or follow the design on dusty old fences" (*GB*, 52). Having arrived at the convent school, the curious and trusting Madeleine looks back at the strangers and shouts, "Don't go away!" (*GB*, 53). But after Madame Severine comes to retrieve her charge, the

A pre-*Madeline* appearance of a tiny redhead with the French name Madeleine.
From The Golden Basket *by Ludwig Bemelmans. Copyright 1935 by Ludwig Bemelmans,*
renewed © 1964 by Madeleine and Barbara Bemelmans. Used by permission of Viking Penguin,
a division of Penguin Books USA Inc.

reader, like Celeste and Melisande, leaves Madeleine behind until the
back cover, where she appears again, dirtying her tiny left glove on an
old stone wall. Clearly, Bemelmans was aware of her charms.

The Golden Basket **and Bemelmans's past.**   The official trip to
Bruges to collect material was not Bemelmans's first. In background
material for *The Golden Basket* that he provided to *Young Wings,* he tells
his young readers that he first encountered the city after a forced landing
on a plane that had gotten lost over the Channel. Ever since he had first
walked through Bruges, he had "wanted to go back there to write and
make pictures for a book—I never knew just why" ("Monsieur
Carnewal," 85–87). Bemelmans concludes that when he did finally
revisit Bruges, he realized that his feeling for the city stemmed from the
many ways in which it reminded him of his childhood in Gmunden, in
Austria.
    Bemelmans's poignant vignette describing these early Gmunden
years, "Swan Country," suggests some of the ways in which his childhood
memories may have influenced the setting of *The Golden Basket.* His
choice of an inn seems a natural one, given his many intimate associa-

tions with the hotel business. Although he apparently wrote about a real inn named Au Panier d'Or (At the Golden Basket),[18] the name may have appealed to him because it recalls the Golden Ship, the name of his father's hotel. Furthermore, in watery Gmunden, as in Bruges, swans were ever present; his father even invented a water-bike in the shape of a swan, and one particularly aggressive bird pushed the youngster in the lake. The frequent downpours of his childhood, which his governess told him were the tears of *"le Bon Dieu"* ("Swan Country," 17, 20), are reflected in the torrents that stream from the Bruges skies during the first half of his story. The watercolors of the book have a muted quality that suggests the light of a rainy day; they recall Bemelmans's observation that "the colors of houses and landscapes mostly in rain sank into my eyes in early childhood" ("Swan Country," 21). Even the chestnut trees of Gmunden are reflected in those which line the Bruges canal, the first of many times when Bemelmans was to grace a picturebook with illustrations of this favorite species.

Apparently Bruges resembled not only Gmunden but also another city of Bemelmans's childhood, Rothenburg, where he had attended school. In a travel article on Bruges for *Vogue,* done at about the same time as *The Golden Basket,* Bemelmans noted that "Bruges is Rothenburg with canals, swans, and house-high chestnut trees" ("Trip," 88).

Perhaps the majestic golden and white steamer of his childhood, the *Elisabet,* which plied the lake with its "phlop, phlop, phlop" ("Swan Country," 8), stimulated Bemelmans's lifelong enjoyment of boats.[19] In any event, the children in *The Golden Basket* love boats, and two whole chapters revolve around activities concerning them: the indoor game of submarine and the outing in the canal. Reveling in one of his favorite subjects, Bemelmans concludes the book with two dramatic drawings of the steamer that takes Celeste, Melisande, and Mr. Coggeshall away from the port at Ostende.

If we may believe his "Monsieur Carnewal" account, a beloved maître d' of Bemelmans's Gmunden days was one of his chief inspirations for *The Golden Basket:* "He is Monsieur Carnewal and with him I started the story" (86). Both the physical description, so carefully depicted in the illustrations, and the gentle personality belong to Monsieur Carnewal: "Over the hotel watched an old *maitre d'hotel,* with a white beard, apple-red cheeks and a small patch of hair which he parted at the back of his head. He always wore a tail-coat, and he often came into my garden to bring me paper to draw on and little stubs of pencils which he could no longer use" (86).

In "Swan Country," identifying the Gmunden maître d' as Monsieur Zobal, Bemelmans notes his amazing facility at folding napkins; this trait also emerges in Monsieur Carnewal, who turns cloth into "swans, windmills, hats, or ships" (*GB*, 26). An evidence of Bemelmans's special feeling for this character is his request to Massee, in his letter from Bruges of 12 April 1935: "I recommend my beloved Mr Carnewal to your good graces, please leave him as much of him as you can [*sic*]."

Perhaps as a child Bemelmans developed his first feeling for the color gold because of its association with his father's hotel, the Golden Ship, or with the steamer *Elisabet,* for which it seems the hotel may have been named. As it approached the dock, the *Elisabet* appeared to young Bemelmans to be "big as a house, alive and floating, snow-white and gold among the lavished wealth of color of garden, field and mountains" ("Swan Country," 8). Clearly the color was a personal favorite: in "Swan Country" he describes the many shades of gold of his favorite season, autumn:

> the rich autumn of the russet and of all the dark reds and umber, the yellow autumn when all the chestnuts trees were lit up with sun, and another phase when the leaves had fallen and the ground was a tapestry of ochre leaves with the trunks of trees turned several shades darker. . . .
>
> Then the last stage of autumn, the park cleared of the ochre leaves, the promenades swept, the trees now bare and the leaves sunk down to the bottom of the lake, shining upward and gilding the water. ("Swan Country," 21)

The color gold appears frequently in *The Golden Basket,* both visually and verbally. Frequently it shines all the more warmly in contrast to a dark frame, as on the front cover, where a golden vista of Bruges draws the eye through the darkened archway of the bell tower and inward to the golden endpapers that expand the aerial view of the city. Finally, on the title page, the eye comes to rest upon the object of its search— l'Hotel du Panier d'Or itself, sketched in brown and covered in a gold wash. Bemelmans's description of dawn associates gold with the sun's light: "The beautiful golden girl stood on her house and showered dusty gold all around her into the young day" (*GB*, 14). Chapter titles include references to a "gold watch," "a goldfish" (*GB*, 16), and "a short sailor with gold teeth" (*GB*, 89).

The adult appeal of *The Golden Basket*.   There is much in *The Golden Basket* intrinsically appealing to an adult. In fact, in "A Trip to

Bruges," a travel article that appeared in *Vogue* at about the time the book appeared, Bemelmans describes and illustrates some of the very same aspects of the sojourn that he incorporates into *The Golden Basket*—the climb to the top of the town carillon, a French general who eats cucumber salad in his room at night, and a chauffeured trip to the port city of Ostende in a constantly overheating car. Furthermore, although Madeleine does not appear by name, convent school girls and their governess also appear. Bemelmans's *Vogue* text comments with typical irony: "The only thing that is not antique in Bruges are these little girls, [*sic*] in orderly rows they wander in and out of churches, and into holy gardens where they are let loose" ("Trip to Bruges," 88).

In *The Golden Basket* Bemelmans uses the same material, but in a manner more appealing to children. For instance, the girls respond as children would to the presence of the French general: they secretly play in his uniform. Not all critics, however, feel that Bemelmans keeps his young reader firmly enough in mind; Peterson and Solt contend that "much of the information included would interest adults more than children" (63). It is true that Bemelmans comes close to ignoring a youngster's attention span and previous knowledge in such passages as the lengthy descriptions of the operation of the carillon or the workings of the inn's kitchen. His description of a master chef at work is at once informative, humorous, and lively adult reading, as is suggested by its inclusion in the Friedes' *La Bonne Table*. But he redeems even this passage, to some extent, with clarifying illustrations and by providing Celeste and Melisande's perspective: in the kitchen, the chef will treat special little girls with raisin cakes, ice cream, and lemon soufflé.

A final appeal to adult readers is the presence of sympathetic adult characters—adults who are both kind to the children and the victims of their gentle tyrannies. In Mr. Coggeshall, the girls' father; Monsieur Carnewal, the maître d'hotel; and Monsieur ter Meulen, the chef and proprietor, Bemelmans provides a focus for his adult readers' own sense of the pleasures and ironies of child-rearing. Mr. Coggeshall, for instance, has carefully rehearsed his lesson on the carillon. He has even drawn a simplified plan of the historic machine's complex workings. But into his pocket it goes when he sees the children standing before the carillon, longing to touch it: "He had enough to do just to watch them" (*GB*, 46). After the bells have boomed, the children race down the stairs ahead of him and begin catching flies in the meat market, thus abruptly signalling to their teacher that the lesson is over.

The Castle Number Nine

In his adult sketch "Lausbub," Bemelmans writes that in his childhood, chief among the 60,000 inhabitants of Regensburg was the Duke of Thurn und Taxis: "He lived in a castle which it took fifteen minutes to pass; it stood in a park that encircled the city. . . . [His] servants wore livery and powdered wigs; he rode about in a gilded coach cradled in saffron leather and drawn by white horses." (12)

Perhaps it was the hold of this elegance upon young Bemelmans's imagination that led him to understand the appeal such a fantasy setting would have for a young reader. In any event, for his third children's book, *The Castle Number Nine* (1937), he departs from the realistic travel fiction model of his first two works and chooses another juvenile form popular then as now—the folk/fairy tale. His own sophisticated product, however, does not so much conform to these norms as parody them. In *The Castle Number Nine* the humor glimpsed occasionally in *Hansi* and seen even more frequently in *The Golden Basket* breaks forth in a continuous stream. The book is a masterpiece of sustained silliness, a romp, a tongue-in-cheek farce made all the more outrageous by the pretended dignity of chapter divisions. Equally remarkable is its innovative integration of pictures and text.

In *The Castle Number Nine* Bemelmans creates two lovable idiots whose complementary character traits provoke disaster. In Melk on the Danube lives Baptiste, a loyal manservant without work whose principal possession is a three-branched candlestick. Answering an ad, he soon begins serving the Count Hungerburg-Hungerburg at the Castle Number Nine in Innsbruck and Hall in Tirol. Here his new master, having decided that certain words are too prosaic for their objects, invents new ones which he insists that Baptiste memorize and use. "Dog" will henceforth be "Friend-on-both-ends," Baptiste himself will be "Bring-me," the bed "Dreambox," the stairs "Leglifter," fire "Happy," the cat "Clawhigh," and the candlestick "Sundrops." One night, the cat, fleeing from the poodle, knocks over Baptiste's ever-present candlestick. Baptiste rushes to the fire chief in the neighboring town and obediently communicates the news of the fire in the new language: "Friend-on-both-ends chased Clawhigh down the leglifter. They knocked over the sundrops which fell in the dreambox and now the whole castle is happy."[20] By the time the laughing fire chief has deciphered and memorized the words, taught them to his men, and returned to the scene of the fire, the castle has burnt to the ground. On the final page, Baptiste, the count, the cat, and the poodle all sit around the remains of the castle, while the count affably announces the story's lesson: "We have learned that in this life one should always call all things by their right and proper names."

Parodying a folk tale. *The Castle Number Nine* is based on a European folk tale of which the English version in Joseph Jacobs's *English Fairy Tales* is entitled "Master of All Masters." In Jacobs's two-page version, a female servant begins work for a new master who requires her to learn nonsense words for various objects. That very night when fire breaks out, the servant awakens the master to alert him to the danger, employing all the new words he has taught her the day before.

From The Castle Number Nine *(New York: Viking, 1937). Reprinted by permission of International Creative Management, Inc. Copyright © 1962 by Ludwig Bemelmans.*

As Jacobs relates the story, the fun lies simply in the repetition of a stream of silly-sounding words to communicate an urgent message: "Master of all masters, get out of your barnacle and put on your squibs and crackers. For white-faced simminy has got a spark of hot cockalorum on its tail, and unless you get some pondalorum high topper mountain will be all on hot cockalorum."[21]

As Bemelmans expands a short folk tale into a 52-page picturebook, he develops the principal characters for comic effect. Jacobs's version devotes no space whatsoever to the servant's personality and only a few words of description—"funny-looking old gentleman" (256)—to the master. On the other hand, Bemelmans devotes most of the first chapter to establishing Baptiste's machine-like personality—mentally slow, precise, and unquestioningly obedient to his late master's wishes regarding the care of his candlestick. When Baptiste and the count finally meet, it is clear immediately that the two are a fated match. The former proudly and incorrectly announces, "I am Hungerburg-Hungerburg and you are Baptiste, and today is Friday." And the methodical Baptiste, referring to his invariable practice of matching the color of his livery to the day of the week, replies, "'When I'm blue it's Monday, sir.' . . . 'How time flies,' said the count."

Bemelmans also enlarges the cast of "Master of All Masters." First of all, he gives the count a poodle, who chases Baptiste's cat immediately after their masters first meet, thus anticipating the second, disastrous occurrence of this action. With the addition of the bumbling fire chief, Bemelmans brings the consequences of the count's mania to their worst possible conclusion. In the original folk tale, the maid communicates the nonsensical message only once, presumably in time to put out the fire. In *The Castle Number Nine,* however, Baptiste must wait in agony as the fire chief memorizes the words and teaches them to his men. The story's logical conclusion is thus markedly different from that of the original: in a final apotheosis, the fire department arrives in time to watch the castle burn to the ground, the towers like candles on a giant birthday cake.

Having expanded this tale, Bemelmans proceeded to put chapter divisions in it, fully conscious of the incongruity of separating such a short text into the formal divisions usually afforded a much longer work. In a letter to May Massee written from the *Santa Clara,* near Cristobal, he acknowledges that "chaptering up a little story like the Castle is a joke."[22] At the top of each chapter, Bemelmans requested underlined arabic numbers like those used in a book by Emil Ludwig,

The Nile, which he thought would add "speed and lift," but at some point, these were instead written out as "First Chapter," "Second Chapter," and so on.

Innovative integration of pictures and text.   As in *The Golden Basket,* the illustrations in *The Castle Number Nine* present an energetic visual variety. Some are in watercolor; others are black and white. The pictures of Baptiste, Count Hungerburg-Hungerburg, and the fire chief are deftly drawn caricatures; in contrast, the illustrations of the three-branched candlestick, Baptiste's album, and his writing utensils are detailed and realistic. Illustrations are playfully framed by partial archways, curtains, mirrors, window shutters, and clouds of smoke.

Bemelmans uses the endpapers to establish the setting, a cockeyed castle with the number 9 prominent on an escutcheon above the door. The castle is surrounded by some of Bemelmans's favorite elements of nature. Swans float in the moat, and his beloved horse chestnut trees, their blossoms looking like nature's own candlesticks, form the picture's left frame. Behind the castle a deer grazes, while in the foreground Bemelmans's skinny-bodied rabbits—precursors of Rosebud and Winthrop—stand about and relax on the lawn. Typically, Bemelmans's illustration invites the eye to linger and examine such details as the activity of each individual rabbit.

On the page before the title page a heraldic shield introduces the narrative's principal elements in a mock heroic fashion—Baptiste, candlestick, cat, poodle, castle, and the fire chief's trumpet. A hearty toast for firemen everywhere, emblazoned in Old English script, establishes the book's inflated tone and piques our curiosity about its outcome: "Give them honor. / Give them fame! / A health to hands / That fight the flame!"

Throughout the book pictures and words interact in an entertaining variety of ways to advance the story. In fact, Barbara Bader describes *The Castle* as "a kind of running picture-story with everything in place" (Bader, 50). As the text begins, the words invite the reader to look at the illustration: "The white house, the second from the left, stood in the little Austrian town of Melk on the Danube." Next the words suggest a second careful look to find the tiny "black cat that can be seen on the roof." On the second page the words and pictures clarify and tease by turns. Pictures help identify such relatively esoteric words as *livery, glossy pumps, wigs,* and *three-branched silver candlestick.* Yet the illustrations are tantalizingly unsatisfying: there are only three liveries and six pair of pumps rather than the implied or stated seven. Furthermore, the three-branched candlestick is depicted in a completely dismantled and virtually unrecognizable state, making this essential narrative element somewhat mysterious at first sight.

Pictures and words also convey the passage of time in innovative ways. For instance, the opening image of the second chapter shows only Baptiste and his cat descending from the carriage that has brought them to the city of Hall. The puzzling text reads, "'Where is the Castle Number Nine?' said Baptiste to four people when he arrived in Hall." A page turn reveals that Baptiste didn't ask all "four people" at once; instead, four illustrations bring the reader step by step to the Castle: "Go over the bridge," directs an innkeeper. "Past the church," says a sentry. "Out of the city gate," a little boy tells him. "And there on the second hill to the right you will find the Castle Number Nine," concludes a shepherd.

When the fire chief finally starts to jump into his uniform, wearing red pajamas and looking like Santa Claus, his disembodied uniform seems to jump gaily with him. Boots, pants, jacket, and helmet all have energy of their own. The words the chief is trying to memorize are written above the jumping clothes—almost as if each word gets one jump, thus suggesting that this jolly activity goes on for some time.

A periodical antecedent.   "The Count and the Cobbler," a piece Bemelmans presented in *Harper's Bazaar* for December 1935, bears a remarkable resemblance to *The Castle Number Nine*.[23] In this double-page spread of 21 illustrations and text, Bemelmans tries out many of the ideas and techniques he developed more fully in the book that appeared a year and a half later. Perhaps he actually worked on the two simultaneously, adapting his formula to the particular requirements of each format. In "The Count and the Cobbler" Bemelmans parodies a French proverb, "A cobbler's childen are worst shod," expanding and reversing it for a happy Christmas story.

The cast of this tale includes Dominik the cobbler, his wife and many children, his "brilliant" baby, and the Count Cesar de la Tour de la Tour Midi, who, incidentally, has a manservant named Joseph. The count orders shoes from the cobbler, who traces the count's foot pattern on a piece of paper. Unbeknownst to the cobbler, his baby then duplicates the act of tracing a foot pattern many times on different sheets of paper. The cobbler, upon finding all these sheets of paper, cannot discern which foot pattern is the count's. Not wanting to disappoint the count, he makes up all the patterns into shoes, with the result that there are shoes to go around. "For once there was a cobbler whose children were shod," and the children go out and sing Christmas carols.

The parodying of a folk tale and the presence of a count with a silly-sounding name are but two of the points of resemblance between this work and *The Castle*. One of the more intriguing similarities is Bemelmans's inventiveness in relating pictures and text to advance his story. For instance, "The Count" begins by drawing the reader's atten-tion to the picture of the cobbler's shop—"In the little house on the right lived Dominik the cobbler"—in much the same fashion that *The Castle* begins. Likewise, as in *The Castle*, Bemelmans subdivides actions into a comic excess of pictures; for instance, "The cobbler worried, and worried, and worried," requires three separate illustrations. Although the cartooning in *The Castle* is far more carefully done, even here simi-larities can be detected; for instance, the tower of the castle of the Count de la Tour de la Tour Midi resembles that of the Castle Number Nine.

The book's making and reception.   Given the resemblance of *The Castle* to the "The Count and the Cobbler," it seems Bemelmans may have begun work on the former as early as 1935. At some point while he was working on *The Golden Basket*, the original *Golden Basket* illustrations were lost in a studio fire.[24] Bemelmans mentions both a fire and *The Castle* in the same undated letter to Massee; thus, it seems likely that work on the two books overlapped.[25] Certainly he had essen-tially finished *The Castle* by the spring of 1937, for during his first trip to South America he sends the last-minute suggestions about chapter headings already mentioned. In a letter to Massee of 21 May 1937 from Quito, in which he discusses both *The Castle* and *My War with the United States*, he seems to be playfully anticipating an award, perhaps the first Caldecott for the former: "I . . . think they'll have to give me the prize, altho [*sic*] I hate that sticker spoiling the jacket."[26] In a letter of 25 May 1937 he refers to his plans for his next book, in which he will "get away from the whimsy of the Golden Basket and the nostalgia of The Castle and write a living, adventurous story." Seemingly, the majority of his work on *The Castle* was finished.[27] (Although it was previously assumed that Bemelmans first received *The Castle* on board ship in July 1937, it now seems that the book he refers to in a letter he wrote back to Viking is actually *My War with the United States*, which was published that same month. *The Castle* did not appear until November.[28])

Although Bemelmans did not conform to the same norms of children's book publishing in *The Castle Number Nine* that he had observed in his first two works, he addressed others. Unlike *Hansi* and *The Golden Basket, The Castle* does not explore the contemporary reality of a foreign country; nor does it have a child character with whom a young reader can identify. Nevertheless, the book makes a number of traditional appeals to young readers. The castle with its moat, the wigs, liveries, and antique appurtenances, as well as the Austrian countryside, all lend the book something of a fairy-tale quality. Furthermore, ending a book with a lesson learned, a moral, is a tradition of children's literature, and this lesson—"We have learned that in this life one should always call all things by their right and proper names"—is certainly one dear to the heart of a child. She herself is, after all, struggling to do just that.

Additionally, *The Castle Number Nine* makes an ironic appeal to adults in ways perhaps unappreciated by children, for, as noted, Bemelmans's treatment of these juvenile norms is parodistic. The very title—*The Castle Number Nine*—suggests a deflation of the usual grand manner in which castles are named, as does a diagram showing mundane domestic details such as a "loose and dripping" tap on the wine barrel and an unfilled vinegar cruet. Except in their manner of dress, Baptiste and Count Hungerburg-Hungerburg are unlike other fairy-tale characters: they are neither exceptionally gallant, clever, nor even evil. They are merely delightfully foolish. And the chaos that results from improper naming results in a disregard for the safe-at-home ending so cherished by juvenile literature; instead, the home is reduced to ash. The lesson about proper naming is wonderfully anticlimactic in the face of such upheaval.

Despite its favorable reviews and Bemelmans's own pleasure in the book, *The Castle Number Nine* apparently did not sell well. (Later he would wonder if this was because "there are no children in it."[29]) On the other hand, Munro Leaf's *Noodle,* which he had illustrated for F. A. Stokes and had come out at about the same time, was a success. In a letter to Massee from Ecuador written in December 1937, Bemelmans expressed his unhappiness over the income generated to that point by his three Viking children's books and *My War with the United States,* noting that "his trade must support a man."[30] He says that "in order to live, I must . . . do another type of book," and informs her of his desire to do a book for F. A. Stokes, entitled *Silly Willy,* seemingly basing it on the seal character who had appeared for the last two years in his weekly comic strip in *Young America:*

With the noodle line, only with my story, be a cartoon book for a price of $1.50 in two colors. I have always had faith in this formula, which I don't think you are fond of very much, a telegraphic text, a stylized cartoon, supplementing the thought, not cheap newspaper cartooning, but somewhat like the jumping of the fire chief into his Uniform [*sic*] picture [in *The Castle Number Nine*].

In the same letter to Massee, Bemelmans mentions that he has other ideas of books he wants to do with her, including another along the lines of *Hansi*. He urges her to invest in him, to support him with a publicity campaign: "My glory need last only ten more years, as long as Mimi is too beautiful to run around in the moribund costumes that are the markes [*sic*] of identification of the wifes [*sic*] of the authors of Childrens [*sic*] books."

Although *Silly Willy* never materialized in book form with F. A. Stokes, Bemelmans's next book for Viking, *The Quito Express*, was itself much shorter than his first two had been. And the desire to go in the direction of "a telegraphic text a stylized cartoon" would lead him finally to *Madeline*. The determination to make his trade pay would guide him into a plethora of creative solutions.

Noodle

In the late summer of 1937, at about the same time that Viking produced *The Castle Number Nine*, F. A. Stokes published *Noodle*, the only children's book that Bemelmans illustrated but did not write. In *Noodle*, Munro Leaf, who had published the classic *The Story of Ferdinand* only one year before, tells another story with an underlying plea for individualism, this one about a dachshund who learns to appreciate himself. One day, as he struggles to dig a wishbone from the ground, the appropriately named Noodle wishes for "some other size and shape."[31] Magically, the dog fairy appears and grants him until that afternoon to decide upon his desired dimensions. After visiting the zoo and assessing the shapes of Mr. Zebra, Mrs. Hippopotamus, Miss Ostrich, and Mr. Giraffe, Noodle marches home for dinner and a nap. Disturbing his rest long enough to see the dog fairy again hovering over him, he sleepily informs her of his decision to remain "just exactly the size and shape I am RIGHT NOW." She praises his "'very wise wish,'" and flies off "with a whirr and a buzz and a flip-flap of wings."

Noodle is dedicated "with affection to the REAL live NOODLE whose superhuman common sense inspired this story," the 11-year-old pet of a neighbor.[32] Bemelmans's stylized illustrations contribute greatly to the appealing characterizations of Noodle and the dog fairy. A comparison of Noodle with the skiing dachshund in *Hansi* shows the extent to which Bemelmans has exaggerated the length of Noodle's body, tail, nose, and ears, as well as the shortness of his legs, thus comically accentuating the qualities which the dog regrets. (Interestingly, in a 1933 cartoon, Bemelmans himself had used the name Noodles for a different sort of long, supple creature—a seal.)[33] The book's format, wider than tall, keeps Noodle's shape in the reader's consciousness. The uneven stance of Noodle's legs and no-nonsense tilt of his head as he walks from one zoo animal to the next create a sense of awkward but determined motion. An illustration adds the humorous bit of information that Noodle takes his nap on a brown couch, his head propped comfortably against a white pillow, thus furthering his characterization as a comfort-loving creature. Leaf's text states that the dog fairy is "a little white dog with wings just like a bird's" and that "she was very polite." Bemelmans's illustration gives the dog a poodle's trimmed head and tail; a smiling, wise face; and large, handlike wings.

Bemelmans's masterful conte-crayon–like illustrations reflect the simplicity of Leaf's narrative structure. Not only are the animals suggested by simple forms, but within the illustrations colors and settings are minimal. With only brown, black, and white, Bemelmans suggests the coloration of the dachshund, the poodle, the zebra, the hippo, the ostrich, and the giraffe. A few brown dots emphasize the text's information that the ostrich is standing in sand, and vertical and horizontal black lines define the "yards" of the other zoo animals.

Bemelmans creates artistic patterns with Noodle's body, varying his compositions in ingenious ways that delight the eye and provide their own forms of visual humor. Noodle's position matches that of each animal in turn; for instance, he stretches out horizontally like the zebra, diagonally like the hippo, and vertically like the giraffe. Around the neck of Miss Ostrich, whose head is underground, he forms a semicircle; and on the last page, his long nose nestling on his even longer tail, he forms a circle around the words "THE END."

Noodle's popularity was such that a quarter century later, Scholastic Magazines published a new version of the book. Although the text in the Four Winds edition communicates the basic story unchanged, in most instances dialogue has been considerably streamlined. Sentences have been shortened and the block of text on the page made narrower so as to make it easier and more inviting to read. Furthermore, in the newer version Noodle's noonday meal is called his "lunch" rather than his "dinner," a change that clarifies the passage of time for the modern reader, inasmuch as the dog fairy has promised to come back in the "afternoon." Unfortunately, some illustrations have been omitted from the non-narrative pages. The newer edition lacks the original endpapers in which Noodle in the lower left-hand corner scratches his ear thoughtfully while looking at the dog fairy hovering in the upper right-hand corner. Also missing is the final page, on which Noodle contentedly curls around the words "THE END."

Quito Express

Bemelmans's next book for children, *Quito Express,* appeared in the fall of 1938, about a year after *Noodle* and *The Castle Number Nine.* In it he returns to the successful travel formula of his first two books, although with a much shorter text and an art style seemingly influenced by his sojourns in South America.

The making of *Quito Express*. In researching *Quito Express* Bemelmans went to South America twice, gathering material at the same time for a number of adult works. After the first trip, a four-month expedition to Ecuador, he arrived back in this country on the Grace Line's *Santa Barbara* on 13 July 1937, with portfolios of photographs and sketches. Only about a week earlier his first adult work, *My War with the United States,* had appeared; the timing of these events resulted in publicity in both the *New York Times* and *Newsweek.*[34] Two months later he sent a message to Viking that said he was sailing "for Chile Saturday noon Wife and Baby,"[35] this time visiting Ecuador, Chile, and the Galápagos. In a letter to Massee in late 1937 he signalled his intent to return in February (25 December 1937). On 31 May 1938 he was off again, this time writing to Massee as he left for Europe on the *S. S. Normandie,* seemingly approving the title: "Quito Express is okay."[36] In the same letter he commented on some Pedro dolls that had arrived from Ecuador and that, presumably, would have been part of a marketing strategy; these were "so bad," however, that he "really saw no hope for them."

Bemelmans's letters from South America show his passionate response to the terrain and its inhabitants as he thinks about the setting and plot for his children's book. At one point he writes excitedly of his

ideas for a story about a steamer that carries equipment through the
Panama Canal;[37] in another letter he talks of gathering material by spon-
soring an essay competition for the Indian children.[38] According to
Publishers Weekly, the story he finally wrote was inspired by an Indian
baby he saw on a train in Ecuador.[39] He describes himself as "in a stupor"
at the incredible beauty of the land, "rich and more beautiful than anything I have seen" (letter 25 May 1937). Upon his return to America,
the *New York Times* quoted him as describing the Otovallo Indians,[40]
about whom he wrote in *Quito Express*, "as the most beautiful physically
of any of the Indian tribes" (14 July 1937).

A book for children.   The plot of *Quito Express*, like that of *Hansi*,
describes a traditional cycle. Home is shown early in the story as the
place where baby Pedro sits in the sun "in front of the little earthen
house,"[41] guarding the drying corn from the greedy chickens. The action
is his four-day round-trip journey. Having crawled aboard the train
called the *Quito Express* in the market town of Otavalo, Pedro is only
later discovered by a kind conductor who puts him to bed in his own
home in Quito for the night. With Pedro aboard, the *Quito Express* makes
a round trip down to the port city of Guayaquil, where it picks up passengers from an ocean liner and then brings them back up the Andes to
Quito. After searching for Pedro's family at every stop past Quito, the
conductor is finally able to return him to his tearful sister, Carmela, at
the station in Otavalo.

As he did in *Hansi* and *The Golden Basket*, Bemelmans communicates
the excitement of travel in *Quito Express*. Every day, when the *Quito
Express* first blows its whistle, Pedro's anticipation causes him to "hop
under his red poncho, and he says . . . 'Dadadada'" (*QE*, 8). As the
story's action begins, Pedro's family goes to market at the Otavalo station. The actual presence of the locomotive—this noisy "big machine"
(*QE*, 14)—causes Pedro such joy that not only does he bounce and gur-
gle, he crawls aboard. Later, aboard the ferry launch of the conductor's
brother in the port of Guayaquil, Pedro is even more ecstatic when he
sees the ocean liner: "He started hopping under his red poncho and said
his loudest 'Dadadadada.' He pointed up to the gleaming white decks of
a big ship, and to the people who came in fine clothes down the side of
the liner" (*QE*, 34). The large and frequent illustrations of the train and
of various boats suggest Bemelmans's thrill at their power and his intu-
ition that children would respond as he did.

The next day Pedro sat in the sun again, and the two chickens were disgusted
because they had thought he was gone for good.

47

From Quito Express *by Ludwig Bemelmans. Copyright 1938 by Ludwig Bemelmans, renewed*
© 1966 by Madeleine Bemelmans and Barbara Bemelmans Marciano. Used by permission of
Viking Penguin, a division of Penguin Books USA Inc.

Quito Express is the third work of Bemelmans's early period with a
clearly didactic intent. Bemelmans begins by locating the land of
Ecuador on a lemon-shaped globe. In the next several pages, both pictures and text depict aspects of the setting—"mountain country and
jungle" (*QE,* 6)—Pedro's earthen house, where one hears the "afternoon
grunt of two little boars with pitch-black wire bristles who sleep in the
shade of the tangerine tree" (*QE,* 10), the pottery his father makes, and
the Monday trips to market, where the donkey "let his ears chase the
flies away and the rest of him fell asleep" (*QE,* 12). Teaching his reader
South American history, Bemelmans depicts the train conductor in his
living room sleeping on a couch "under the picture of Simón Bolivar,
who was the liberator of South America" (*QE,* 29). And, as he did in
Hansi and in *The Golden Basket,* Bemelmans includes foreign words—
Ferrocarril (railroad [*QE,* 22]) and *Pobrecito* ("poor little fellow" [*QE,* 33]).

The tone of *Quito Express,* like the ubiquitous sun, is smiling and
warm. Furthermore, touches of caricature enliven this relatively tension-

less story. For three pages of the train ride, two Indian women sleep and awaken by turns, with dancelike synchronization, on either side of Pedro. When both wake up at the same time, "each one thought that Pedro was the son of the other, and both of them said to themselves: 'What kind of mother is that one, with such a little boy? / And she does not feed him!! / Or hold him on her lap! / But lets him sit on that hard bench!'" (*QE*, 18–19). The two women glare, their eyes the only motion on the page, each condemning the other. In another image, the unsympathetic station master, a "stern man" (*QE*, 24), looks ridiculous with hat pulled low over his glowering eye, hawk nose, and mass of dark facial hair. The compassionate but inexperienced conductor lugs Pedro around under his arm like a sack of flour. And his brother, the effusive skipper of the *Gloria*, is so caught up in Pedro's problems that "he had to steer the *Gloria* with his shoe, because he needed his hands to listen to the conductor" (*QE*, 33).

Adult appeals.   The genial, illustrated presentation of information about a foreign country may make *Quito Express* appealing to an adult reader. Critic Ann T. Eaton, who had found all of Bemelmans's books to be enjoyable adult fare, again noted that this book "will be as much fun for the adult who reads it aloud as for the children who listen."[42] Perhaps, however, the strongest appeal for the adult reader is the way the book engages his sense of protectiveness. Pedro's long absence from home is alarming to anyone reading the story, especially to those old enough to sympathize with Carmela. The conductor's obvious concern for Pedro's plight and efforts to return him to his family direct the reader's response: Pedro needs help! And yet Pedro himself, like Madeline to come, is blissfully unaware of any danger, delighting in new sights and sounds.

A new illustrative style.   Bemelmans's illustrations for *Quito Express* mirror his Ecuadorian subject matter both in medium and in drawing style. The brown tones of what appears to be sepia conte crayon on coquille board suggest the earthen houses and earthenware pottery of the Indians. Reflecting an art style "new to him but old to the Indians,"[43] Bemelmans uses simple geometric figures to depict human shapes, thus anticipating *Madeline*. Pedro's pancho and straw hat form two triangles separated by a rectangular face. Similarly, the sarape-draped Indian women on the train resemble wooden dolls.

A number of reviewers expressed some concern over the appropriateness of the art style for a children's book. May Lamberton Becker described the pictures as "at first somewhat baffling but soon capturing the affections."[44] Louise Seaman Bechtel said that "the usual child does not like the full page pictures, in my experience," but concluded that "there should be inspiration for the young artist in the ease and strength of these sophisticated sketches."[45] The critic for the *New Yorker* sarcastically attacked the art style as incomprehensible to a child: "The drawings reach such a peak of naivete that we were called upon to interpret them to a seven-year-old, who couldn't for the life of him make out the artist's picture of a hen."[46] Ignoring those who found his work too sophisticated, Bemelmans would soon go even more dramatically his own way, sure of his universal appeal with *Madeline*.

Chapter Three

Madeline and the Sequels:
The Making of a Classic Series

Madeline

In 1939, only five years after his first book, Bemelmans published *Madeline,* a work that won the Caldecott Honor Award the next year and that has achieved classic status as it continues to thrive in one format or another more than a half-century later. "Classic" here means a work that reaches a wide audience and stays in print for a long time. A number of factors account for this kind of success. This chapter will explore *Madeline*'s creation, the book's initial appeal, the development of the series, and Bemelmans's marketing efforts. Chapter 5 returns to the question of what makes a classic, examining ways in which *Madeline* is still modern.

Madeline's plot deals humorously and deftly with serious childhood concerns—a brush with death and going to the hospital. After opening lines that are among the most famous in picturebook history—"In an old house in Paris / that was covered with vines / lived twelve little girls in two straight lines"—the daily routine is established: "In two straight lines they broke their bread / and brushed their teeth / and went to bed."[1] Against a backdrop of famous Paris sites, the little girls and their trusted governess, Miss Clavel, walk "in rain / or shine." Soon we learn that Madeline is the smallest, the bravest, and the one most likely to cause alarm. Naturally, it is she who, "in the middle of one night," has an appendicitis attack, culminating in an ambulance ride and an emergency appendectomy. As Madeline continues to improve in the hospital, Miss Clavel and the other 11 girls visit her, where they see "toys and candy / and the dollhouse from Papa." Upset with the attention Madeline is receiving, the little girls return home and disturb Miss Clavel's sleep for a second time. Discovering that they have no serious cause for alarm, Miss Clavel tells the girls to go back to sleep. "And she turned out the light— / and closed the door— / and that's all there is— / there isn't any more."

The making of the book: going off on his own. Bemelmans told the audience who had gathered to give him the 1954 Caldecott for *Madeline's Rescue,* the second *Madeline* book, that his own early boarding school experiences as well as stories of his mother's convent school provided the inspiration for *Madeline*'s setting:

> Her beginnings can be traced to stories my mother told me of her life as a little girl in the convent of Altoetting in Bavaria. I visited this convent with her and saw the little beds in straight rows, and the long table with the washbasins at which the girls had brushed their teeth. I myself, as a small boy, had been sent to a boarding school in Rothenburg. We walked through that ancient town in two straight lines. I was the smallest one, but our arrangement was reversed. I walked ahead in the first row, not on the hand of Mademoiselle Clavel at the end of the column. ("Acceptance," 256)

The inspiration for *Madeline*'s plot came during a summer vacation on the Île d'Yeu off France, a vacation that, according to Madeleine Bemelmans, was *"definitely* during the *summer of 1938."*[2] A year later in a chapter of *Small Beer* entitled "The Isle of God," Bemelmans described a biking accident that landed him in a "small white carbolicky bed" in the hospital, noting that in varying light the crack on the ceiling over his bed "looked like a rabbit, like the profile of Léon Blum, and at last, in conformity with the Island, like a tremendous sardine."[3] He mentions only briefly that "in the next room was a little girl who had had her appendix out." (*IG,* 161). Less than two weeks after the August 28 publication of *Small Beer,* however, as *Life* magazine for 4 September 1939 previewed *Madeline,* it noted that Bemelmans had been "so impressed by the enjoyment that the child derived from her operation that he decided to write a children's book in which the heroine should experience a similar adventure."[4] Years later, to his Caldecott audience, he further elaborated upon his experience, mentioning "the stout sister that you see bringing the tray to Madeline, and the crank on the bed," and finally describing what is perhaps the book's seminal and most famous scene: "standing up in bed, with great pride she showed her scar to me" ("Acceptance," 257).

Although Viking acquired the rights to *Madeline* in 1958, May Massee initially declined the work. Years later, Bemelmans, in a letter to Dr. Kerlan of the University of Minnesota library, noted that "my own publishers the Viking Press turned it down."[5] Madeleine Bemelmans also has written that "May Massee . . . turned down *Madeline,*" pointing out that afterwards it was "promptly accepted" at Simon & Schuster.[6] Massee doubtless viewed the work with its brief text and cartooned images as inappropriate for children. Certainly Bemelmans knew that this was not what she wanted: he had even said so in his letter to her from Quito the year before.[7] But as he said at the time, "I have always had faith in this formula."

It seems, too, as if Massee may have thought the book with its large, full-color pictures would be expensive to produce. Only the year before *Madeline*'s publication, *Publishers Weekly* reported that Bemelmans "likes to work on a large scale," so that "the picture can come flowing out as he wants it to be" ("Humor," 1510). The article noted, too, that "the only quarrel he ever has with Miss Massee, he says, arises because he usually tries to persuade her that children's books should be three feet square," a difficult idea for her to accept "considering production problems" and the fact that books have to fit on shelves.

Years later, Bemelmans greatly exaggerated his difficulties in getting *Madeline* published: "Nobody wanted to publish it. . . . They said it was too sophisticated for children. Of course, I never in my life wrote for children. I write for myself. But finally Simon and Schuster took it, after it had been sitting in a drawer for five years" ("Madeline's Master," 115). His later assertion notwithstanding, a letter received by May Massee's office on 15 December 1938 clearly shows that by this date Bemelmans had already sold *Madeline* to Simon & Schuster:

> Madeline has just become the child of Simon and Schuster and Bemelmans, I am going to try an experiment that I have always wanted to try—to shoot pictures and text "Bang Bang Bang" I would only like you to know that I feel a little bad about it, not because they have taken it, thats [*sic*] good, they are the Ideal people for that book, and because— well its [*sic*] too hard to explain, at any rate it will widen the market this year with Stokes doing Silly Willy in April, and Simon and Schuster Madeline in October.[8]

Clearly, Bemelmans was now pursuing the ways of making his trade pay that he had outlined to Massee in his letter from Quito the year before (25 December 1937). He still expected to do a Silly Willy book with F. A. Stokes, although this was never to materialize. And taking *Madeline* to Simon & Schuster would have the positive effect of further broadening his base. Nevertheless, he no doubt felt some regret, and perhaps some uncertainty, at doing a book without the benefit of his mentor's encouragement and expertise. He goes on in this letter to Massee to talk of plans for their doing other books together and even to suggest that he would appreciate her advice on *Madeline:* "If I have my little girls ready, I will bring them in to you, hope you will give it your strictest critisism, [*sic*] will you do that?" (received 15 December 1938).

In "The Isle of God (or Madeline's Origin)" Bemelmans states that he made the first sketches for the book in Paris at the Restaurant Voltaire and wrote "[t]he first words of the text . . . on the back of a menu in Pete's Tavern" in New York.[9] In *Young Wings*, he wrote that he did the "draft" at Pete's the year after the Île d'Yeu vacation,[10] a time frame that suggests that he did so with his commitment from Simon & Schuster already in hand.

Years later, in 1958, Viking purchased the rights to *Madeline* from Simon & Schuster. By then they had published *Madeline's Rescue* (1953) and *Madeline and the Bad Hat* (1957). Shortly after the transaction, Bemelmans sent Massee a postcard depicting Madeline in a Parisian flower market on one side and the note, "Congratulations from Madeline's father" on the other.[11] Clearly he was glad the book had come back to her care.

The original Simon & Schuster format was 23.25 cm x 31 cm, a generous page for Bemelmans's paintings. For its part, Viking, after purchasing *Madeline* from Simon & Schuster, at some point pared one-half centimeter from the original format. Although as tall as the original *Madeline,* the currently published Viking *Madeline* books are only 22.75 cm across; both side margins have accordingly been narrowed. The visual effect, particularly in two facing full-page colored pictures such as "in rain / or shine" is to crowd the two slightly in the gutter (the inside margin). As a result, the book moves just a bit faster, urging the eye on from page to page, rather than inviting it to rest on each separate picture.

Madeline's first appearance.

Madeline conforms to a number of the important trends and traditions affecting juvenile literature in the late 1930s. At the same time, from its first appearance, the work appealed strongly not only to children but also to adults. The editors of *Life* magazine must have foreseen this likelihood: shortly before the book appeared, the issue for 4 September 1939 included a condensed version of *Madeline* and a brief article about the book's creation. The magazine presented 15 of the pictures and enough of the rhyming text to tell the whole story. *Life*'s venture was successful: in a review of *Madeline* for the *New York Herald Tribune,* May Lamberton Becker wrote that "Madeline has appeared to great applause in a stylish magazine for grown-ups."[12]

Life states that *Madeline* was scheduled to be published on 5 September, in fact, the very next day after the magazine's publication date. (Murray Pomerance, however, observes a disparity between this and Simon & Schuster's publication date of 15 September [Pomerance, 306].) In any event, the book was soon out and an immediate hit. Becker was not the only reviewer to note *Madeline*'s success with readers of all ages. Writing for the *New York Times*, Anne T. Eaton praised its many virtues "for children 6–8, and for readers of any age who love Paris."[13] Josephine Smith exclaimed in *Junior Libraries,* "If children have a chance to see it, they will like it. So far, the adults seem to have been enjoying this story. . . . 'For goodness' sake—read *Madeline!*' "[14]

Bemelmans's statement that he wrote for himself, not for children ("Madeline's Master," 115), must of course be taken with a grain of salt. Under Massee's tutelage, his earliest works, especially *Hansi* and *The Golden Basket,* had been shaped by her standards of juvenile publishing. By the time he started *Madeline,* however, Bemelmans was ready to express his own unique vision of a picturebook. Perhaps one reason for his success with adults lay in the fact that, while many of the techniques he used were relatively innovative in children's picturebooks, they were already well received in adult art and literature.

Madeline as a children's book.   Like *Hansi, The Golden Basket,* and *Quito Express, Madeline* clearly has its roots in the picturebook publishing trend of the 1930s that introduced young readers to foreign countries. Where it differs significantly in this regard from Bemelmans's first books is the extent to which the didactic role is assigned primarily to the illustrations. In the earlier works, Bemelmans both explains and shows; here he primarily shows, by depicting famous sites and the daily activities of Parisians. This instructive function was originally announced on a dust jacket: "Its heroine as you will see, lives in a place pronounced Paree; which gives you quite a splendid chance to learn the ways of Paris, France."[15] On the back dust jacket, a list of the settings was provided; sometime later this list was incorporated into the book's last page.

Madeline contains a number of elements reminiscent of the folk tale, which by the 1930s had long since become a staple of the juvenile library. *Madeline*'s famous first lines—"In an old house in Paris / that was covered with vines"—establish the setting with traditional brevity. That Bemelmans does not say "when" *Madeline* occurs introduces a hint of timelessness and fantasy into an essentially realistic story. Similarly, the last lines—"and that's all there is— / there isn't any more"—have the ring of a typical folk-tale ending.

The narrative structure of *Madeline* and the sequels is likewise traditional. The movement follows the much-used cycle of leaving and returning home: at the story's outset 12 little girls emerge from the "old house in Paris"; by the story's end they are safely tucked into bed. Furthermore, *Madeline* is shaped by the repetition of actions and phrases. For instance, each time Miss Clavel awakens to trouble, the words read, with slight variations, "In the middle of one night / Miss Clavel turned on her light / and said, 'Something is not right!'" Perhaps Bemelmans's recent success as illustrator of Munro Leaf's *Noodle* (1937), in which the dachshund's quest is built around a series of nearly identical dialogues with the zebra, the giraffe, the hippopotamus, and the ostrich, influenced his decision to use the technique in *Madeline*.

To some extent, the "twelve little girls in two straight lines" recall the presence of unnamed or undifferentiated protagonists such as those of Boris Artzybasheff's *Seven Simeons: A Russian Tale* (1937), Claire Bishop's *The Five Chinese Brothers,* illustrated by Kurt Wiese (1938), or Wanda Gág's *Snow White and the Seven Dwarfs* (1938). In *Madeline* the 11 little girls do not act individually, as anonymous characters sometimes do in folklore; however, their group unhappiness and rebellion dominates the book's closing pages.

Bemelmans's use of rhymed couplets to narrate *Madeline* is yet another way in which he followed accepted practices of children's book publishing. As noted, his fondness for nineteenth-century German picture story artist Wilhelm Busch may have influenced his choice of this technique, which he had himself employed at times in "Thrilling Adventures of Count Bric a Brac" and in "Silly Willy." By the 1930s and 1940s, nursery rhymes, songs, and other forms of poetry had long been recognized as desirable for children and were a popular source of material. In *Madeline* Bemelmans's imperfect verse bounces and jiggles along, contributing to the book's gaiety. It is one of the work's greatest appeals, as even young children can quickly memorize it and "read" it back with the aid of pictures.

Finally, *Madeline* resembles other books of the 1930s and 1940s in that its prevailing ambience is one of security. This security, so tantalizingly stressed by the dangerous nature of Madeline herself, is assured first of all by the many icons of law, medicine, and religion—the *gendarmes,* nurses and nuns, Paris's massive churches, and other official-looking buildings. In fact, Bemelmans notes that he had in mind "the great patriot and humanitarian," Léon Blum ("Acceptance," 257),

Socialist premier of France from 1936 to 1938, in depicting the doctor, Madeline's dedicated rescuer. Above all, security is represented by the ever-present, sweetly smiling Miss Clavel, whose very shape suggests the Virgin Mary.[16] Frequently Miss Clavel stands in the center at the back of the line or in the approximate middle of a cluster of girls, indicating by her position that she is the unifying force. On the final page, with her line arms outstretched on either side as she prepares to draw closed the dormitory's double doors, her stance approximates the image of the cross on the wall above her head. Centered on the page, Miss Clavel's image suggests that, despite Madeline's disruptive absence, peace will be restored.

Even though her presence is reassuring, Miss Clavel leaves something to be desired as surrogate mother. The black robes that enclose her form dehumanize her. Although she weeps sadly when Madeline leaves for the hospital in the doctor's arms, she seldom holds, kisses, or feeds her. These very shortcomings, however, make Miss Clavel a perfect catalyst for Madeline's own popularity: the perceived emotional distance leaves a void that intensifies the reader's sense both of Madeline's independence and of her vulnerability.

A second way in which Bemelmans establishes a sense of security is through a predominance of symmetrical structures, both visual and verbal. In an article entitled "On the Problem of Symmetry in Art," Dagobert Frey writes that "symmetry signifies rest and binding, asymmetry motion and loosening . . . the one formal rigidity and constraint, the other life, play, and freedom."[17] The symmetrical layout of illustrations, the frequently repeated image of "twelve little girls in two straight lines," and the rhyming couplets all establish an underlying sense of control.

Still a third way in which Bemelmans reassures his young readers is by reminding them of his presence as author, of subtly reminding them at crucial moments that the book is simply that—a book. Initially, he invites them through the frame of the endpapers, suggesting that they are entering a different world. As Bemelmans presents the drama of pain and separation that forms the emotional core of the book, his insistence on the illusion of his art holds his young reader at a safe distance. Madeline's departure in an ambulance from the safety of her house forms the story's climax: "In a car with a red light / they drove out into the night." The resolution follows immediately on the right-hand side of this same double-page spread: "Madeline woke up two hours / later, in a room with flowers." Bemelmans's sudden switch to full color in this spread after the yellow wash of the immediately preceding pages not only signals the arbitrariness of his means of representation but also permits him to communicate speedily a positive resolution; for from left to right, the setting changes dramatically from night to day, from dark to light. Furthermore, his sudden shift from the relatively distant perspective of an ambulance riding through the streets of Paris to Madeline's close-up view of the flowers at her bedside diverts attention from the fact that Bemelmans, in conformance with one of the bylaws of children's literature, has spared the young reader the frightening sight of the appendectomy.

As Bemelmans brings *Madeline* to a close, he again reminds the reader that his book is illusion. His voice visibly disappears as the print size diminishes through each of the last four lines, momentarily drawing attention to the arbitary and malleable nature of this means of representation. With the words "That's all there is— / there isn't any more," the narrator emphasizes that Madeline's world has been, after all, only a story.[18]

Special appeals to adults.   In selecting Paris as the setting for *Madeline,* Bemelmans chose a foreign city with a unique appeal to adults. With World War II in progress, Paris was of interest to all Americans as an imperiled heart of Western civilization. In fact, France entered the war against Germany on 3 September 1939, only the day before *Madeline* appeared in *Life* magazine. Nine months later France surrendered, remaining under Nazi rule for the next four years, until 25 August 1944.[19]

In the face of the occupation, Bemelmans's vision of Paris as a gay, charming, and safe place must have created a sense of longing in contemporary readers. As Edward Koren wrote 46 years later in a *New York Times* review of *Madeline's Christmas,* the Paris of the *Madeline* books is "a belle epoque Paris, unchoked by automobiles or crowds. . . . It is a Paris of leisure, grace and charm—where Madeline and her entourage can stroll in two straight lines across the Place de la Concorde without any murderous automobiles bearing down on them to disrupt their symmetry and order."[20] Just as *Madeline*'s early readers could enjoy Paris as they wished it to be rather than as it was, so, too, could they imagine in the perfect regularity of the boarding school life a continuance of European civilization. So well known in this country was the image of orderly schoolgirls that in its issue for 9 September 1939, when the *New Yorker*'s "Talk of the Town" column sadly discussed Britain's entry into the war (on 3 September), the bottom of the page was illustrated with a double line of uniformed school girls, all wearing gas masks.[21]

Even before the war, Paris was of special interest to sophisticated Americans as a center of fashion and the arts. Traveling for *Vogue* publishers Condé Naste in 1938, Bemelmans published "Ah, Paris!" a full-color double-page spread of drawings of Paris, with an accompanying text full of the intimate pecularities of French daily life.[22] In October 1945 *Vogue*'s American war correspondent, Lee Miller, elatedly cabled news of the Liberation and promised to resume coverage of the fall couture collections.[23]

Not only does *Madeline* feature a city of special interest to adults; the full-color illustrations are done in an expressionistic art style that was currently popular. The best-known artist to practice this style, in which figures are delineated in pen or ink on a background of wash, was French artist Raoul Dufy (1877–1953). Dufy's work appeared a number of times in American magazines; for instance, he did covers for *Town and Country* for January, February, and May of 1937.[24] Although Bemelmans's *Madeline* illustrations are derivative, they are nevertheless uniquely energetic, humorous, and gay. Furthermore, inasmuch as the full-color illustrations serve the didactic and narrative aims of imparting information about Paris while advancing the story, they are more representational than many Dufyesque paintings.

In using an expressionistic art style, Bemelmans thus appealed to at least a certain segment of adult readers. At the same time, by his own account, he seems also to have expected children's acceptance of this style. In his Caldecott acceptance speech, he notes that he "wanted to paint purely that which gave me pleasure, scenes that interested me; and one day I found that the audience for that kind of painting was a vast reservoir of impressionists who did very good work themselves, who were very clear-eyed and capable of enthusiasm. I addressed myself to children" ("Acceptance," 256). Much earlier, in its April 1942 issue, *Vogue* had reported that among the many furnishings of Bemelmans's Gramercy Park apartment was a large painting of the New York waterfront done by six children of Hartley House ("Ludwig Bemelmans' Splendide Apartment," 61). Writing in the introduction to the catalog for his 1959 exhibit of scenes of New York, Bemelmans acknowledged the pleasure he found in this work "of astonishing power . . . that has been mistaken for a Picasso and also, I am flattered to say, for my own work. . . . [I]t gives me joy whenever I look at it."[25] Thus, despite the fact that most children's book editors in the late

1930s sought a more representational style, Bemelmans must have been confident that children themselves would find a kindred spirit in his approach.

Yet another currently chic fashion in art made its way into Bemelmans's illustrations. Trompe l'oeil ("fool the eye"), a technique of drawing furniture, bird cages, and other real objects on the wall, had come back into popularity at just about the time *Madeline* appeared. Only about six months earlier, *Vogue* described a revival of interest in this decorating trend, picturing elegant drawing rooms in London and Paris with illusionary corners, statuary, curtains, and framed "pictures" surrounding niches holding real objects.[26]

This revival, in itself, would seem to owe much to the ontological preoccupations of artists of the early twentieth century. Picasso, for instance, between 1912 and 1914 experimented with techniques such as collage—which brings fragments of the real into the illusionary—and dramatically framed pictures within pictures.[27] As noted, Bemelmans himself had long engaged in trompe l'oeil décor, painting furniture and objects on the walls of rooms. This same playfulness over illusion and reality finds its way into *Madeline*'s endpapers, where a framed and labeled picture of the 12 little girls crossing the Place de la Concorde is hung not on a wall but apparently out of doors, against a backdrop of leaves, thus making the reader question the reality of both the picture and the trees. Two photo spreads devoted to Bemelmans's Gramercy Park apartment show that he had decorated his own walls with a similar leafy pattern: typically, he was rearranging reality in his personal environment, in this case bringing the outside in.[28]

Yet another way in which Bemelmans addressed *Madeline* to accepted adult tastes was in his use of cartooning. In his letter to Massee, Bemelmans had stated his faith in such an approach, "which I don't think you are fond of very much" (25 December 1937). According to Barbara Bader, Massee's view was shared by many editors, who thought such art to be less than the best that ought to be presented to children (Bader, 2–12). On the other hand, by the time *Madeline* appeared, comic strips and cartoons had achieved great popularity as adult entertainment in newspapers and in magazines such as the *New Yorker* and the *Saturday Evening Post*. Comic historian Maurice Horn notes that in America by the end of the 1920s, the comics were nearly as popular as the movies (*World Encyclopedia of Comics*, 20). Here again Bemelmans no doubt knew that even though librarians and book editors might not approve of comics for young readers, the children themselves loved them, then as now.

Madeline represents the culmination of Bemelmans's evolution toward a cartooning approach to the picturebook, both in the use of a nonrepresentational style and in a low ratio of text to pictures. Although the human figures in *Hansi* and *The Golden Basket* reveal some detail and modeling, in *Madeline,* as in *Quito Express,* they become little more than flat geometric shapes. Miss Clavel, for instance, suggests an elongated Modigliani figure, while the girls are comprised of circular faces atop triangular bodies. And although Bemelmans relies more heavily on illustrations in *The Castle Number Nine* and *Quito Express* than he did in *Hansi* and *The Golden Basket,* not until *Madeline* does he achieve the ratio he describes in his Caldecott acceptance speech as "very little text and . . . a lot of picture" ("Acceptance," 256). The illustrations alone convey the physical reality of life in the "old house in Paris," of the other 11 little

But the biggest surprise by far—
on her stomach
was a scar!

girls, and, most important, of Madeline herself and her relationship to the others. Only Bemelmans's deft drawings show the saucy tilt of her chin, her red hair, and the fact that she stands apart.

In addition to his illustrative and storytelling approaches, Bemelmans's fondly ironic treatment of the values of the little girls has a special appeal to adults. As Madeline proudly displays her scar, and later, as the 11 other little girls cry, "Boohoo, / we want to have our appendix out, too!" only the adult reader can fully appreciate the naïveté of the little girls' jealousy, being able, through experience, to judge that such attention is not worth risking danger and pain. The adult caretaker can sympathize with the trials and tribulations of Miss Clavel—the book's most frequently depicted character—and can share her relief when the final "disaster" proves to be no more serious than it is.

Madeline's personal appeal to young and old.   Perhaps the single most important reason for *Madeline*'s classic status is the appeal of the main character to both children and adults. She stands saucily alone, her red hair demanding attention. To a child, Madeline is the daring role model, the archetypal picturebook heroine. Ethel Heins describes her as "the naive but stalwart child . . . the kind of strong, individualistic personality young readers found abundant in the past, such as Little Tim, Harold (of the purple crayon), and the anthropomorphic Peter Rabbit, Curious George, and Ferdinand" (Heins, 58). Adults too, enjoy a character who, like Bemelmans himself, will not conform; she flaunts life's dangers, yet she winds up enjoying special privileges and attention.

At the same same time that Madeline appeals to a reader's delight in successful nonconformity, she evokes sympathy for her isolation from her biological relatives, a situation shared to a lesser extent by all of Bemelmans's earlier protagonists. Her parents are never pictured, and the only reference to their existence is a tantalizing mention of "the doll-house from Papa." Both young and old feel concern for her vulnerability.

The name Madeline is an English version of Madeleine, the name of Bemelmans's wife, although according to her, "he always called me 'Mimi'" (letter of 31 July 1988). Madeleine is also the name given to his daughter at her christening; however, not long afterwards, and sometime before the appearance of *Madeline* in 1939, the latter's name was changed to Barbara. Barbara was two during the vacation on the Isle of God and three the year *Madeline* was published. A picture of her on a donkey in France, presumably from the Île d'Yeu trip, appears in the *Life* magazine article (4 September 1939, 7). Thus, to some extent,

Bemelmans may have had his own toddler in mind as he wrote, but she was only one of several sources of inspiration. In a *New York Times Book Review* interview in 1993, Barbara Bemelmans commented that her father had said his famous protagonist "was a little bit of his mother, a little bit of my mother, and a little bit of me."[29] Bemelmans had already given the French name Madeleine to the little red-headed Belgian convent school boarder in *The Golden Basket* (1936), a book that had its roots in his honeymoon trip and which appeared in the year his child was born. Clearly, although the little girl Bemelmans met in the island hospital after his accident may have suggested *Madeline*'s plot and thus inspired him to begin working on the book, Madeline's beguiling character resembles not only that of this child but also that of other Madeleines, both fictional and real.

The fact that Madeline is assigned no particular age contributes to her appeal. In its issue for 14 November 1960, *Publishers Weekly* commented, "To most children she generally seems to be whatever age they are when they first discover her, and this is likely to be long before they can read."[30] Bemelmans's drawings of Madeline provide no consistent cues as to her age. At times, he varies her height to suit the emotional content of the picture. For instance, when she alone defies the tiger while the other girls cower around Miss Clavel, her short stature emphasizes her bravery. When she shows off her scar, she looks much taller, when compared to the zoo picture, than even normal stretching would account for.

The Viking Series

Following a hiatus of more than a decade, Bemelmans returned to the adventures of his charming progeny with *Madeline's Rescue*, which won the Caldecott in 1954. In the next eight years, Viking published three more books in the series: *Madeline and the Bad Hat* (1957), *Madeline and the Gypsies* (1959), and *Madeline in London* (1961). At the time of his death in 1962, Bemelmans was at work on yet another *Madeline* book, an expansion of *Madeline's Christmas*, which had earlier appeared as a book insert in *McCall's* for 1956. The *McCall's* work was finally published in the standard Viking format in 1985.

Capitalizing on *Madeline's* success, each book in the original series followed the formula of the first. In each, the same cast of characters explores foreign turf. Each story is framed by a standard opening and closing, related in irregular rhymed verse, and illustrated with a combination of full-color expressionistic watercolors and cartooning. Each book opens with framed endpapers. The series was good for sales, for as *Publishers Weekly* commented in 1960, "the appearance of a new book about Madeline always stimulates sales of the previous titles" (17).

Madeline's Rescue. Clearly Bemelmans realized *Madeline*'s adult appeal, for with the exception of *Madeline and the Bad Hat,* he printed all of her adventures in adult periodicals before publishing them in book form. So it was that *Madeline's Rescue* made its first appearance in *Good Housekeeping* in its "Best and Happiest Christmas Issue" for December 1951. The work is listed in the extensive table of contents of "the magazine America lives by" under "Stories and Features," not under the "Children" section, and was thus obviously intended for older readers as well as young (2). A year and a half later, in the spring of 1953, Viking published the hardcover edition. Soon afterwards, in June, Bemelmans treated the readers of *Collier's* magazine to a short sequence entitled "Madeline at the Coronation."[31] The timing of this double-page color spread, in which Madeline and entourage go to England for Queen Elizabeth II's coronation, surely increased interest in the book. The next year, the critics gave *Madeline's Rescue* the Caldecott Award, thereby ensuring renown and sales in the children's market for years to come.

With many minor differences in the verse, the *Good Housekeeping* "Madeline's Rescue" conveys the entire story used later in the book (55–60). The presentation consists of 31 illustrations, numbered in sequence and spread across five pages. Instead of yellow wash, a variety of accent colors—yellow, orange, green, and blue—are used sparingly.

In expanding the magazine version into the book, Bemelmans added the full-color illustrations of Paris, thus enhancing the work's esthetic value and informational content.[32] On the cover, an unusually subdued little Madeline is carried in Miss Clavel's arms across the Pont des Arts. Someone new to Madeline's world, a dog, follows along behind, and for once, Madeline is not wearing her hat, which another girl carries for her. This image, combined with the book's title across the top, suggests the aftermath of a successful rescue. The symmetrical centering of the bridge and the solidity of the Institut de France in the background convey a sense of orderly resolution.

Bemelmans uses the endpapers both to continue the drama of the cover and to suggest events to come. A framed picture presents a dramatic aerial perspective of the Seine. Boats flow up the page on the left and down on the right. Bridges cross the river from foreground to background; on the Pont des Arts in front are the 12 little girls and Miss

Clavel. Clearly, time has elapsed, for now the same brown dog, wearing a red bow, heads up the double-line formation rather than following it. This second watery image again hints at the nature of the "rescue" while piquing the curiosity of those who knew the first *Madeline* book. Who is the dog? and what will it do in the story?

Madeline's Rescue proceeds from crisis to crisis, with the rescue of the title being quickly effected within the first eight pages. In the earlier book, Madeline had displayed the naughty habit of frightening Miss Clavel by walking along the bridge railing. Now, the logical consequence finally ensues: she falls into the Seine. A mutt saves her and soon becomes the beloved school pet, Genevieve. Six months later, the school trustees arrive for their annual inspection and, creating the second crisis, turn Genevieve out into the streets. After an exhausting search through all of Paris, the girls return without their dog. Late that night, Genevieve shows up and, admitted by Miss Clavel, goes back to bed with Madeline. The little girls begin to fight over the dog, and, awakened for the second time that night, Miss Clavel announces that Genevieve will have to leave if the girls can't settle their differences. Still a third time, Miss Clavel "turned on the light" (*MR,* 53), when a little girl summons her to see Genevieve's solution to the problem—12 puppies: "Suddenly there was enough hound / To go all around" (*MR,* 55–56).

In creating the plot of *Madeline's Rescue,* Bemelmans combined two basic ideas—falling into the Seine and losing a dog. In his Caldecott acceptance speech he describes the second half as coming first, and attributes the idea to two little girls, the daughters of author Phyllis McGinley, to whom he paid "fifty cents apiece if they would give me an Idea, for I was paralyzed with lack of imagination" ("Acceptance," 258). After receiving their money, the children promptly offered this suggestion: "There's a dog, see—Madeline has a dog. And then the dog is taken away but it comes back again, maybe with puppies so all the girls can have dogs." Continuing, Bemelmans relates that one day, the story came together for him as he watched the much-loved mutt of a Parisian clochard:

> An object was floating down the Seine, and little boys ran along the quay, and as the object came near it turned out to be an artificial leg. One of the little boys pointed at it and said, *"Ah la jambe de mon Grand-père!"*
>
> At that same moment a long line of little girls passed over the Pont des Arts, followed by their teacher. They stopped and looked, holding onto the iron rails with their white-gloved hands. The leg was now very

close, and the dog jumped into the Seine and retrieved it, struggling ashore and pulling it from the water by backing up the stones.

There suddenly was a great vision before me. The plot was perfect. ("Acceptance," 258–59)

As Bemelmans relates the story here, he describes the rescue sequence depicted in the book, with the important exception that it is Madeline who is rescued, not "my grandfather's leg." Elsewhere, however, he relates the moment of inspiration somewhat differently. A year earlier, for *Young Wings,* he had written simply:

I used to take long walks along the river Seine, and my dog liked to run down and swim in the river. One day as I sat there, some little school-girls, exactly like the little girls in your book, passed in a long line. They crossed the bridge that is called Le Pont Royal just as they did in your book. Then the idea for the story came. I walked to another old tavern. It overlooks this bridge and is called Le Restaurant Voltaire. After lunch I asked the waiter for a menu. I turned it over and wrote: "And nobody knew so well how to frighten Miss Clavel until the day she slipped and fell." And that was the start of your story, *Madeline's Rescue.* (13)

The versions differ in at least three ways—the owner of the dog, the name of the bridge (the Pont des Arts in one and Pont Royal in another), and, most important, the fact that Bemelmans suggests he witnessed a kind of rescue scene in one but not in the other. Bemelmans knew well that a little boy screaming *"La jambe de mon Grand-père!"* would provoke the laughter of the adults hearing his Caldecott acceptance speech. On the other hand, in the account written for the members of the Junior Literary Guild, he emphasizes his attachment to his dog—an attachment heightened in *Young Wings* by a picture of their shadows together in the Tuileries. In fact, it seems that either story—or neither—may be true. As early as 1947 Bemelmans had recognized the comic potential of a Seine rescue, minus the dog, when he illustrated his short sketch "#13, Rue St. Augustin" with a black and white image of a Paris *gendarme* racing with a pole to fish someone out of the river.[33] The suspicion that even at the moment of accepting the Caldecott Medal Bemelmans was not being entirely "truthful" makes one attend to Madeleine Bemelmans's words of caution: "I would like to state emphatically that much of what Ludwig wrote or said in interviews was a blend of fact and fiction—not for purposes of deception but to make a good story" (letter to author, 31 July 1988).

The near-drowning sequence reveals Bemelmans's expressionistic use of color. As Lyn Ellen Lacy points out, these pages reveal an indebtedness to fauvist painters André Derain and Maurice de Vlaminck.[34] (Madeleine Bemelmans notes that De Vlaminck, along with Georges Braques and Paul Klee, were among the artists admired by Bemelmans [letter of 31 July 1988].) In the book's first double-page spread, Bemelmans paints both the sky and the Seine an oppressive yellow, thereby heightening a sense of anguish as the police attempt their rescue (*MR*, 10–11). In the next full-color picture in this sequence, the river is a muddy green, realizing the words "a watery grave" (*MR*, 14). Finally, in the picture of Miss Clavel carrying Madeline home (a repeat of the front cover), the sun, which had been glowing yellow in the two previous pictures, is a deep red, suggesting the intensity of the moment in which innocence is first shaken (*MR*, 15). Significantly, this full-page illustration bears no words, the effect being that the emotion of the moment cannot be expressed in Bemelmans's light-hearted verse but must be left to the more powerful visual medium.

For his young audience, Bemelmans uses a number of techniques to make the rescue sequence exciting without being terrifying. The first, of course, is to signal the rescue's success on the book's title and cover page. Then, as the accident unfolds, *gendarmes,* passersby, and boaters are everywhere, offering lines and long hooks. The heroic pup is a solid-looking creature. Furthermore, even though submerged up to her nose, Madeline looks slightly silly, certainly not tragic. The fact that she still wears her hat and gloves while in the water suggests that she has not lost her fundamental identity; these come off only when she is safely in Miss Clavel's arms.[35] Soon she is home in bed with the protective canine, being offered, like her equally adventuresome predecessor Peter Rabbit, a cup of camomile tea.

The six pages devoted to the second crisis—the annual school inspection—provide a good example of Bemelmans's use of caricature to relieve a terrifying situation (*MR*, 26–31). Through images and words, Bemelmans shows the trustees to be at once imposing and ridiculous, frightening and silly. As types, they exemplify those professionals described by Henri Bergson in *Laughter* in whom we see *"the letter aiming at ousting the spirit. . . .* Constant attention to form and the mechanical application of rules here bring about a kind of professional automatism."[36] The trustees devote their corporate energy to the ousting of one small dog. Their hearts have taken leave, and all that remains is adherence to discipline: "Isn't there a rule / That says DOGS AREN'T ALLOWED IN SCHOOL?" (*MR*, 28).

Bemelmans's use of perspective distorts the trustees, making them loom threateningly toward the reader, as they emerge from the limousine and then progress through the dormitory for the inspection (*MR*, 26–27). Visual details suggest wealth, heartlessness, and power. Beads, top hats, fur pieces, ascots, and stick pins imply wealth. One trustee wears a dead animal with the eyes apparent—a clear sign of a machine where there ought to be a heart—and two of them carry what are, in essence, sticks—an umbrella and a cane.

And yet at the same time that the trustees are threatening they are also comic in the Bergsonian sense, rigid and "out of it." They all look barely capable of walking: two lean on canes and umbrellas, while the limp arms and slack legs of the one emerging from the limousine suggest a marionette. Their eyes stare straight ahead, glazed and unresponsive (*MR*, 26).

Bemelmans's language, too, emphasizes the mechanical, the nonhuman. As the trustees totter from the car, the text reads, "For on that day there arrived a collection / Of trustees for the annual inspection" (*MR*, 26). The very word "collection" suggests something nonhuman, perhaps rocks, trading cards, or butterflies. The language of the trustees is stilted, artificial, and perfectly accented by rappings of their sticks: "'Tap, tap!' 'Whatever can that be?' / 'Tap, tap!' 'Come out and let me see!'" (*MR*, 28).

The sorrow of the search is alleviated by the interest of the details that Bemelmans includes in the scenes of Montmartre, les Halles, the church of Saint Germain des Pres, and Père Lachaise Cemetery (all identified on the book jacket). In the Tuileries readers are treated to a humorous and fascinating double-page spread filled with pictures of dogs and owners of every description—a tweedy Englishman with a bulldog, a rich couple with three trimmed poodles on leashes, and a sheik with an Afghan, to name only a few. There are big dogs and little, spotted and plain. Even the marble huntress Diana races with her hound. But alas, no Genevieve (*MR*, 38–39).

In his review of this and other of Bemelmans's works, *Saturday Review* critic Lee Rogow observed that in the world of "Bemelmania . . . dogs . . . have the nobility and charm of perfect knights" (Rogow, 13). Certainly this is true of Genevieve, who, despite her being a "creature of uncertain race" (*MR*, 30), heroically assumes the other characters' burdens. First of all, she dives into the water to rescue Madeline, and she succeeds where others fail. Then, after the heartless trustees have cast her out and Madeline and Miss Clavel have despondently given up the search, she returns home on her own. (Critic Shelton Root finds Miss Clavel's contrasting "ineptitude" during this same sequence to be potentially upsetting to the child reader.[37]) Finally, Genevieve settles the problem of her ownership by producing one puppy for each girl. As another of Madeline's surrogate parents, Genevieve represents a more physical kind of motherhood than that represented by Miss Clavel: she snuggles close, and she creates abundant new life.

Madeline's Rescue has humorous, action-filled, and visually intriguing colored pictures of Paris, including two double-page spreads, the first time Bemelmans used this larger display in a *Madeline* book. The lost dog plot, suggested by the daughters of Phyllis McGinley, has an intrinsic interest for children. Despite these values, however, the book is not as completely pleasing as the original *Madeline*. The plot lacks the relative simplicity of the first; its most compelling crisis is resolved at the outset, and the book wanders without a sense of climax from then on. The work also lacks the graceful and calm closure of the first; instead of showing everyone safely home in bed, it reveals the projected moment when Genevieve and her pups will accompany Miss Clavel and the 12 little girls on a walk. In other words, although everyone is physically inside, the illustration shows them going out, thus jarring a sense of symmetrical rest. Finally, the illustrations are not as pleasing. The cartoons themselves lack the gray outlines that give those of *Madeleine* a distinct soft, full quality. Barbara Bader points out that the drawings and the paintings do not complement each other as well as in the first book: "When the drawing [in *Madeline's Rescue*] becomes cruder and more cursory [than in *Madeline*], the painting more dense and detailed, the illustration suffers as such and the total design falls apart" (Bader, 51).

Perhaps *Madeleine's Rescue* deserved the Caldecott; on the other hand, perhaps the committee was primarily acknowledging the quality and continuing popularity of the first work and somehow compensating for the fact that it had not received the highest accolade in 1940. In any event, with the Caldecott in hand, interest in all *Madeline* books from then on was virtually assured.

Madeline and the Bad Hat.

In December 1956, the same month that *Madeline's Christmas* came out in *McCall's,* Bemelmans's next Viking sequel, *Madeline and the Bad Hat* appeared in a special edition, with the trade edition following in March 1957. The limited autographed edition was sold for $7.50 at the Hammer Galleries; at the same time, the gallery presented "Paintings, Drawings, and Sketches" for this book as well as for *Madeline's Christmas*.[38] In another multipronged attack, Bemelmans continued to widen his market. The book received the *New York Herald Tribune* Children's Spring Book Festival Award in 1957, an accolade that further served to enhance the growing prestige of the series.

According to an article entitled "Author-Artist," Bemelmans thought about *Madeline and the Bad Hat* for about five years: "I made over a thousand sketches for it and about six dummies, complete with varying illustrations and text, until finally I came to the version which is in the book."[39] In 1954, in his Caldecott acceptance speech, Bemelmans spoke of his plans for a book involving "Pepito, the son of the Spanish Ambassador who lives next door to the little girls and is a very bad hat" ("Acceptance," 259). He noted, too, that he had been to Spain three times looking for a model for Pepito and his house. In "Author-Artist" Bemelmans relates that he at last found the boy he was looking for in his own godson, Italian Marc Antonio Crespi. The article noted, however, that "the real boy is very different from Pepito . . . for he loves animals, especially rabbits." Madeleine Bemelmans, on the other hand, has written that she could not provide a photograph of Pepito because he "was not a real live boy" (letter of 5 September 1994). Perhaps, as in the case of Madeline herself, there was no single inspiration for the character, but several.

In *Madeline and the Bad Hat* Bemelmans places at the heart of the conflict a subject that he alludes to throughout his writings for children and adults—kindness to animals. As early as 1937, in "Poor Animal!" he had expressed disgust with the cruelty of bullfighting in Ecuador.[40] Seven years later, in 1944, he made a drawing of domestic and wild animals entitled "Speaking Out against Vivisection" to be used "for the cause." After Bemelmans's death the Vivisection Investigation League offered reprints of the picture suitable for framing to the readers of *Town and Country*.[41] Apparently Madeleine Bemelmans shared his love of creatures, for Bemelmans asked that the limited edition be dedicated "To Mimi and her menagerie with love."[42] (The dedication was, however, shortened to "To Mimi," in both the limited and the trade editions [Pomerance, 119].)

Unfortunately, Pepito's desire for attention reveals itself not only in very antisocial behavior, but also in mistreatment of animals. First of all, he makes ugly faces and shoots his slingshot at the girls as they exercise in the garden. He scares them, shocks them, and knocks them over. Then Pepito reveals even worse tendencies when he catches and cages neighborhood animals and invites the girls over to see "my menagerie— / My frogs and birds and bugs and bats, / Squirrels, hedgehogs, and two cats."[43] Trying to impress the girls, he dresses up as a matador, but Madeline rejects these efforts and expresses Bemelmans's view of bullfighting when she announces, "A Torero / Is not at all our idea of a hero!" (*MBH,* 22). Once Miss Clavel has given Pepito a tool kit as an outlet for his energies, he horrifies them all by building a guillotine to chop off the chickens' heads: "He ate them ROASTED, GRILLED, and FRITO! / Oh, what a horror was PEPITO!" (*MBH,* 28).

In the first climax, Pepito's cruelty undoes him when the cat he had slated for the dogs' plaything jumps on Pepito's head in terror, and the boy finds himself fighting an angry pack of mongrels. Having saved the cat while Miss Clavel was saving Pepito, Madeline responds to Pepito swathed in bandages in a most unloving fashion, telling him, "It serves you right, you horrid brat, / For what you did to that poor cat" (*MBH,* 42). This stern reprimand has a comic result: "And lo and behold, the former Barbarian / Turned into a Vegetarian" (*MBH,* 44–45). Now Pepito's kindness is immoderate: after releasing all the animals in his own menagerie, he walks around the zoo releasing exotic birds, kangaroos, and elephants. Just as he nears the lion cage, in the book's secondary climax, Madeline approaches him and, putting her arm around his neck, assures him that "He was no longer a BAD HAT. / She said, 'You are our pride and joy, / You are the world's most wonderful boy!'" (*MBH,* 52). At home that night, the girls and Pepito wave at each other through the window as all "brushed their teeth and went to bed" (*MBH,* 53).

As he does in all the *Madeline* books, Bemelmans uses the front cover, endpapers, and title page to introduce key elements of his story. Using a technique common to the comic strip, he gives Pepito identifying headgear—a remarkable tall black hat decorated with two red pom-poms, which, he notes in "Author-Artist," is based on "those he had seen in Spain." On the front cover, Pepito doffs this hat gaily as his bike splashes water on the dismayed little girls at the Place de la Concorde, thus establishing his character as the problem. In the framed picture of the endpapers, the girls observe a mysterious-looking Pepito in a black cape as he fishes beneath a bridge near Notre Dame. Bemelmans uses the title page to suggest the book's resolution. Madeline holds a bouquet of lilies of the valley, a traditional French offering of friendship, while Pepito, wearing a loin cloth, happily shows off by raising a barbell, a behavior harmful to neither man nor beast. One foot "tames" the stone lion of his garden wall; he has learned to approach lions only in jest.

In painting *Madeline and the Bat Hat,* Bemelmans treated his readers to the colors of his favorite season, autumn. The vines that cover the old house and those that frame the first picture are golden, and the trees in Pepito's garden as he releases the animals in his menagerie are russet and yellow and shades of brown and dark green. Likewise, the lion, an animal that appears with relative frequency in Bemelmans's picturebooks, is tawny; perhaps the creature's color is one reason for the artist's predilection for it.[44]

One of the book's most arresting double-page spreads (there are eight) is an expressionistic depiction of Pepito happily atop the roofs of Paris, sailing a kite "in the autumn wind" (*MBH,* 14–15). Brown and yellow leaves swirl across a yellow sky, energizing a uniquely tranquil moment in Pepito's life. In the background the major churches of Paris—Sacré Coeur, Notre Dame, and the Madeleine—all offer their protection to the carefree boy, as does a crucifix on the wall in the room barely visible just below.

The principal climax shows Bemelmans's skill both at building suspense and at offering his young readers a quick resolution to a life-threatening situation. He begins with three double-page spreads that distance the reader from Pepito, heightening interest in what he is doing. On the first of these, way over to the right, Pepito's small figure appears in a crowd of Parisians enjoying the Bois de Boulogne. Clad in black, he carries "a bulging sack" (*MBH,* 31). As the reader and the girls trail after him curiously, on a second double-page spread, "He was followed by an increasing pack / Of all the dogs in the neighborhood" (*MBH,* 32–33). Both color and design of the third double-page spread suggest a catastrophe, belying Miss Clavel's naive interpretation: "That boy is simply misunderstood. / Look at him bringing those doggies food!" (*MBH,* 34–35). The little girls in the foreground peer at Pepito in the distance, still in black, still carrying a mysterious sack, attracting dogs like a magnet pulling iron filings. The yellow sun burns intensely. Finally, on the next two pages, the action breaks loose in four small pictures. From the bag, Pepito releases a cat, which jumps on his head, and soon Pepito is buried beneath the dogs. This time Bemelmans does not draw out his "Miss Clavel to the rescue formula" with a series of pictures to prepare for a comic letdown as he did at the conclusion of *Madeline.*

Instead, he heightens a sense of real danger by rushing her to the scene in the last image of these two pages. Immmediately after a page turn, the text announces her success: "She came in time to save the Bad Hat, / And Madeline took care of the cat" (*MBH,* 38). Just in time! One of the dogs is about to chomp down on Pepito's metonymic hat.

In focusing *Madeline and the Bad Hat* on the reformation of Pepito, Bemelmans, of necessity, changes Madeline's character slightly. She is not the one who needs to be rescued—the one to be rushed to the hospital or fished from the Seine. For the first time, she is not the major problem; rather, she saves the cat, and later, just in the nick of time, saves Pepito from his folly. Bemelmans keeps her character naughty in her unsympathetic treatment of the severely injured Pepito, but he permits her to reveal exceptional maturity in understanding his need to be accepted in the final sequence at the zoo.

Madeline and the Gypsies.   *Madeline and the Gypsies* (1959), the next Viking sequel, treats readers to Madeline and Pepito's gay adventures while traveling around France with a gypsy circus. This is the first *Madeline* book to appear after Bemelmans and Viking agreed with Simon & Schuster in 1958 to bring *Madeline* itself back to the Viking fold. Perhaps Bemelmans's dedication of the book to May Massee thus expresses his continuing appreciation for their long alliance.

The book begins with Pepito inviting Madeline and the little girls to a gypsy carnival. A violent rainstorm leaves Madeline and Pepito at the top of a Ferris wheel, a fact that Miss Clavel realizes only after the gypsies have rescued the pair and carried them away in their wagon. In this gay escape from routine, the children travel all around France, soon learning to perform all manner of circus tricks. As soon as Madeline sends a postcard to Miss Clavel, the distraught guardian comes in great haste; but, glimpsing Miss Clavel's arrival in her crystal ball, the Gypsy Mama hides Madeline and Pepito by sewing them inside a lion's skin. Although happy enough in their new role, the children quickly realize that they are in great danger of being shot when they venture outside of the circus. Upon their return to the arena, they see Miss Clavel and the other little girls in the front row. Despite the sobs of the gypsy circus members, Madeline and Pepito go back to Paris and (almost) routine—a bath, clean clothes, and two straight lines of beds for acrobatics. On the last page, Miss Clavel enters the dorm with a flashlight that she beams on Madeline: "And then she came back, just to count them once more!"[45]

Madeline and the Gypsies was first introduced in abbreviated form as a 16-page book insert in *McCall's* December 1958 issue and was advertised as "a *McCall's* Christmas gift for the whole family."[46] Although the magazine version tells the entire story, nearly every illustration varies slightly from those used later in the book. Eight of the illustrations are in full color, but except for the cover picture itself and one double-page spread of the Gare St. Lazare, none of these appears in the book. Furthermore, most of the lines of verse were changed slightly.

The most obvious addition to the book version are the scenes of France through which Bemelmans continues his exciting geography lessons for readers of all ages, as Madeline and Pepito tour the country from north to south and back again. Framed endpapers depict the two children on the back of a plumed horse looking over the Pont d'Avignon in a scene gay with pink and white trees. In one of several double-page spreads devoted to famous sites, the massive Mont St. Michel, named after heaven's own warrior angel, protects the children during their complete separation from home and family, subtly emphasizing a sense of security. Furthering the book's didactic purposes, a list of the scenery is provided on a final page.

One of Bemelmans's neatest feats in *Madeline and the Gypsies* is to depict what is basically a kidnapping without making it terrifying. Madeline and Pepito have a wonderful time in their escape from the routines so well established by the famous verse of the three preceding *Madeline* books: "How wonderful to float in a pool, / Watch other children go to school, / Never to have to brush your teeth, / And never— never— / To go to sleep" (*MG,* 20–23). The Gypsy Mama, the Strong Man, the Rouault-like clown, the elephant, and the horse all form a happy family into which the children are admitted with great affection. Learning to perform tricks is wonderful fun, and leaping through the lion tamer's hoop is the most exciting of all: "This was a fascinating game. / Compared to this, all else was tame" (*MG,* 34). Bemelmans's consciousness of the importance of this more delicate treatment is shown in the changes he made after the magazine version, in which the Strong Man locks the children in a cage after the Gypsy Mama sews them into the lion suit.

In depicting the kidnapping as relatively safe, however, Bemelmans created a Gypsy Mama who is neither clearly villainous nor clearly loving. She weeps and smiles as she gives the children "potent medicine" (*MG,* 16), tucking them into bed as the caravan prepares to leave Paris.

And, at the point when Miss Clavel and the little girls rush by car and train "to the scene of the disaster" (*MG,* 30), the reader has no real sense that the happy children are involved in a disaster of any kind; instead, the phrase serves as the motivation for a humorous variation on the visual formula, as the car—not Miss Clavel herself—races to the scene, front wheels lifting off the ground. True, the Gypsy Mama tricks the children into putting on the lion skin once she sees Miss Clavel coming in her crystal ball, and at this point the reader feels uncertain about the Gypsy Mama's motives. The book's text doesn't clarify if she wants to keep Madeline and Pepito because she loves them or, more selfishly, because she needs them in the circus. At the moment when the children find Miss Clavel in the audience, the magazine version offers the reader the former reason, stating, "Because she had no children of her own, / And now these two were as good as gone" (*McCall's,* n.p.).

Furthermore, Madeline's motivation in writing to Miss Clavel is vague. After 10 glorious pages of enjoying the carefree circus life without so much as a mention of her governess, she says, "It's about time / We sent dear Miss Clavel a line" (*MG,* 28). The postcard says, "Dere Miss Calvel We ar in a cirkis and feeling fine—Mush love vrom Pepito and Madeline" (*MG,* 28). Seemingly, she does this out of affection or a sense of obligation; nevertheless, her decision to write is so abrupt that one views the letter as the author's device to precipitate the crisis of Miss Clavel's arrival.

Madeline and the Gypsies is marred at times by limp verse. In a passage such as the following, Bemelmans moves so far from the underlying beat that his imperfect rhymes slip into formlessness: "Poor Miss Clavel—a shadow of her former self / From worrying, because, instead of twelve, / There were only eleven little girls— / Stopped brushing their curls / And suddenly revived / When the postal card arrived" (*MG,* 29).

Madeline shows some development as a character in this sequel. At the outset she is, as ever, "the smallest one" (MG 5). And in the first incident the reader can infer that she is less brave than Pepito, who climbs down from the Ferris wheel in order to bring help to her. Once she and Pepito join the circus, however, she becomes more independent and physically more sturdy than ever before. Often she wears an outfit like Pepito's—form-fitting harlequin tights—and performs acrobatic tricks on horseback without fear and without falling. And it is she who thinks to write Miss Clavel. Nevertheless, for the adult reader, she still functions as Miss Clavel's special problem; somehow caring for Madeline is always uniquely challenging.

Bemelmans's love for animals no doubt influenced him to choose the circus as setting. He presents the black steed in several full-color images, the horse's strength all the more reassuring—and thrilling—in contrast to tiny Madeline and Pepito seated on his back. On another double-page spread, Bemelmans uses a series of tiny line drawings of the children learning to ride, thus suggesting in one layout the passing of many days. The ever-present elephant, a benevolent gray mass, helps rescue Madeline, performs in the show, and, in a humorous touch of personification, weeps into a handkerchief when the children prepare to leave. Capitalizing on the fearfulness of the king of beasts—as he had also done in *Madeline and the Bad Hat*—Bemelmans gets a number of laughs from scenes of the "lion" sending farmers and hunters running for cover as the children roam the Normandy countryside.

Although *Madeline and the Gypsies* has flaws of character motivation and moments of weak verse, its basic subject expresses a zest and a sense of freedom unmatched by any of the other *Madeline* books. The plot is perhaps too farfetched for the work ever to touch the sympathies of a young reader in the same wrenching way that *Madeline* or *Madeline's Rescue* does; nevertheless, in *Madeline and the Gypsies* Bemelmans has appealed to every child's fantasy of escaping from school and joining the circus.

Madeline in London.   Bemelmans spent a great deal of time and energy in the composition of *Madeline in London,* which first appeared in a full-color *Holiday* magazine spread in August 1961. The magazine heralded the feature with a front-cover illustration—not used in the book—of Madeline and Pepito on horseback.[47] Later that same year the Viking edition appeared. By now Bemelmans had a strong sense that the *Madeline* books would endure, and he wanted to make this work worthy of future readers. As he wrote to Massee on 11 October 1960, "I am conscious that in the matter of Madeline, we are working for all time and that the story and the pictures must be as perfect as I can make them."[48]

Madeline in London is typical of Bemelmans's plots in that it presents a series of minor crises rather than one long built-up action. The story begins with Pepito and his family moving to London, where Pepito soon becomes ill and starts to waste away, so much does he miss his Parisian playmates. His father, the Spanish ambassador, invites Madeline, Miss Clavel, and the other little girls to their residence in England. As a birthday gift, the girls present to Pepito a horse that has been retired from the

Madeline in London

by

Ludwig Bemelmans

From "Madeline in London," Holiday, *August 1961. Reprinted by permission of Madeleine Bemelmans.*

Queen's service. Upon hearing a trumpet blast, the horse bolts to take his old place in the Queen's parade, bearing, of course, Madeline and Pepito. The parade marches through much of London, with Miss Clavel and the girls running after. That night, forgotten during the birthday festivities, the old horse eats up the embassy garden and becomes violently ill. After the vet revives him, Pepito's mother regretfully says the horse can no longer stay. Madeline takes the *equus non gratus* back to Paris, where "They brushed his teeth and gave him bread, / And covered him up / and put him to bed."[49]

In moving Madeline from her native land, Bemelmans continued to pursue the same didactic goal of the previous books, sparing no effort to depict faithfully every physical aspect of London. To Massee he wrote that "this must be, while like the other books, different, for that thing which is London, the architectural severity, yet cosiness, the precision of the various types, uniforms and the gear for horses, all must be correct" (11 October 1960). To Marcel Salinas, an assistant who was collecting sketches for him, he wrote on 29 October 1960 a "list of the objects I need—especially the harness, stable stuff—the lights and trucks at London airport—official lettering—LONDON TAXI—to get the feeling that this is another city than Paris . . . that it is LONDON."[50]

By his own varying accounts, Bemelmans spent two or three years on this kind of research, getting the feel for life itself that he viewed as essential to successful illustration. On the same day that he wrote the list to his assistant, Marcel, he also wrote to Lord Edward Stanley, enclosing a short outline of the book and noting that he had "taken two years thinking about this."[51] He asked for Stanley's help, apparently in getting permission to "hang around the Horse guards and get the smell of leather and animals, the routine, the proper terms, the proper gear etc. The language of London cavalry men." In another letter written only a couple of months later, he commented that he had been "thinking some three years in images on this book, looking at London, sketching London, going through books[,] photographs, doing at least a thousand sketches."[52]

A picture such as the double-page spread of Miss Clavel and the girls crossing the street bears witness to the use of this kind of research: the clothing of the bus attendants and passengers, the bobby, the taxi driver, the gentleman in the bowler hat, and the Buckingham Guards, as well as the double-decker bus and the architecture of the palace, the shop, and the restaurant are faithful to the originals. The text, too, teaches an English custom: "Look right before you cross the street" (*ML,* 23). With similar fidelity, Bemelmans depicts such well-known sites as London Bridge and the Tower. While individual aspects of London may be faithfully reproduced, however, Bemelmans makes no attempt to move his action from point to point in a sequence that would literally have been possible within the time frame; as he did in the other books, he moves his action around the city (or in the case of *Madeline and the Gypsies,* around all of France) without scrupulous regard for the actual proximity of the various locations.

Bemelmans's letter to Salinas, in which he seems to be thinking aloud to himself—for he admits that "I really write this to myself"—offers valuable insights into his vision of what kind of art pleases a child. He clarifies what is, for him, a crucial difference between essential fidelity and boring precision: "Please be very careful about this—while we want detail it must not be weary detail—it must also not loose [*sic*] the vision

of the child which gets deadly bored by the absence of entertainment—
we must not clutter the thing with architectural detail, or for the sake of
being correct count the buttons on every guardsman."

In a postscript he clarifies that he wants each page turn to stimulate
the child's eyes and mind: "When I say the boredom of the child—I
mean a lack of surprises—. I should like to have evry [sic] page turned a
challenge to its eyes—and to the mind." His letter shows, too, his clear
conviction that children appreciate art that resembles their own efforts:
"It must all be there BUT and so that the child feels—that it could have
made the picture him, or herself—that is as you know the result of
either being a child yourself or else of working and doing five hundred
sketches until the cramp leaves your hand, your eye and your mind—
and suddenly there it is" (29 October 1960).

Although nothing about the picture of Buckingham Palace just
described approaches photographic realism, it nevertheless offers a myr-
iad of interesting bits of information that intrigue and thus inform a
child. Faces—circles with a few dots and lines for features—appear in
each window of the double-decker bus; some people read papers, and
everyone is wearing a hat, except for two children who peer out the back
window. The man in the bowler hat is carrying an umbrella and staring at
other hats in a shop window. The guards walk stiff legged, carrying bayo-
nets and wearing enormous black hats. On the far right side, diners can
be seen on the ground floor of a restaurant. The buildings are geometric
masses of red or brown with the essential architectural details quickly
sketched over in black, white, and yellow. The picture is original and
highly informative without being boring. Clearly, Bemelmans's work,
childlike in some ways, was the intentional product of insight, careful
research, and intense effort on the part of a highly accomplished artist.

The majority of the actual work on the book was done between the
late fall of 1960 and the early spring of 1961, when he wrote to Viking,
"So here it is 3 P.M. the 4th of March 1961 and this book is done."[53]
Textual revisions continued into the summer. By now the popularity of
Madeline was such that Bemelmans had barely begun on Madeline in
London when he sold it to Holiday magazine, which looked at the
sketches and bought it "on the spot for a fat price and will run it coming
summer on six pages in color which makes it a wonderful ad to 1 million
people for us."[54] On 30 November 1960 Bemelmans wrote requesting a
room at Claridge's in London with northern exposure and a used carpet
that wouldn't be bothered by ink stains, noting that an assistant, Marcel
Salinas, would be working with him.[55]

Six weeks later Bemelmans had hit an unexpected snag: his work was suddenly looking like "whiskey ads, traveling posters or 'Come Visit England' throw aways" (13 January 1961). Bemelmans's solution was "always, to go back and look at it with fresh eyes, so I have locked all the soldiers and parade stuff that was; [*sic*] away, and rearranged them in new formations" (13 January 1961). Although it cost him five days' work, the effort was worth it, for one of Bemelmans's finest accomplishments in *Madeline in London* is to present London's well-known visual identity in new ways. For instance, he keeps a uniformed parade before the reader for 10 pages without ever permitting the subject to become trite or boring. In one double-page spread, he uses an oriental calligraphic style to depict the parade in the background while long-necked cranes in the foreground look on. Other scenes avoid a traditional look through their intimacy, gaiety, humor, choice of details, and variety of perspectives.

In his letter to Salinas, Bemelmans emphasized that he wanted to surprise the child:

> NEVER TO FALL INTO ROUTINE—for example there should be pictures that you don,t [*sic*] expect. Like in the Spanish household—the Chef making a huge birthday cake and the help around it as he writes on it with pink sugar HAPPY BIRTHDAY PEPITO, in Spanish—should say that it is Pepitos [*sic*] birthday—*not a statement of that fact in print*—Children always love to see *something to eat, thats {sic} sweet*. (29 October 1960)

Pepito's birthday provides both the occasion for the horse and the occasion for the cake. Although the book in its final form does not include the picture Bemelmans describes in his letter, it does present a wonderful scene of all the children in a kind of gay and fantastic dance around the finished product (*ML*, 38). Presenting "something to eat, thats sweet" was something Bemelmans had intuitively done in children's books since the *Lebkuchen* of *Hansi*.

Bemelmans's dictum "NEVER TO FALL INTO ROUTINE" also helps explain his motivation to vary his verbal and visual formulas throughout the *Madeline* books. The formulas are there, offering the reader the security of known story structures. But the variations intrigue a reader's mind and eyes, especially if one knows the previous books as points of comparison. For *Madeline in London,* rather than offering a multicolored view of the story's setting, the endpapers present an expressionistic, solid-red picture of London; the tail of a plane bearing the lit-

tle girls breaks the frame, seemingly entering the picture. The mind is
engaged immediately in understanding that only six little girls—not
12—can peer through the six windows on this side of the plane, and
that the other six girls are there, unseen. The opening page of *Madeline
in London* presents the most elaborate presentation yet of the familiar
setting and characters: each of the 12 little girls holds up a piece of paper
on which is presented a story element, including the "old house in Paris,"
"at half past nine" (represented by a grandfather clock), and "Pepito"
(shown in his pom-pom hat) (*ML,* 5). The image of the two rows of beds
(*ML,* 11) has been moved to a rich red room at the ambassador's London
residence. It is the gardener's distress that elicits the formula "Everybody
had to cry. / Not a single eye was dry" (*ML,* 45), first introduced in
Madeline and the Gypsies when the children leave the circus. It is the gentle horse who goes through the routines of having his teeth brushed and
being put to bed by 12 little girls, in pictures filled with fascinating
details. Even the last page contains a surprise: the cutaway view of the
old house now shows not only the girls' dormitory, but also the floor
below, where sleeps the horse, his head on a pillow. The final two lines
reflect the change: Miss Clavel "turned out the light and closed the door.
/ There were twelve upstairs, and below one more" (*ML,* 56).

As in earlier *Madeline* books, kindness to animals is an important
theme in *Madeline in London.* Pepito's horse is originally acquired from a
stable to which he had been retired after active duty with Her Majesty's
Forces. As the little girls adopt and then bathe him, the text comments
on the unfortunate fate of others not so lucky: "Some poor old dobbins
are made into glue, / But not this one— / Look, he's as good as new"
(*ML,* 16). As he began work on the book, Bemelmans wrote to Paris
requesting that his sketches (presumably for this book) be sold and that
the money be given to the English and Irish societies "that buy up horses
to prevent their shiping [*sic*] to France for butchery."[56]

Apparently, he at first intended to give the horse a name, for he wrote
to his assistant to collect a dozen horse names at the "horse guards bar-
racks. Should be a boy suggest weight, monumental qualities" (29
October 1960). Ultimately he did not name the horse, perhaps because
he could not find anything he thought would stand the test of time—
"for this is forever" (29 October 1960). In dealing with the subject,
Bemelmans wanted "to avoid stickyness [*sic*] and sentimentality" by
choosing "horses of quality, *not victims*" (29 October 1960). Accordingly,
Pepito's pet has dignity: he is "gentle, strong, and sound" (*ML,* 15). On
the title page the horse appears rock solid, facing forward with Madeline

and Pepito balanced one on either side. Yet he is so gentle that a little girl can tie a bib around his neck and kiss his nose goodnight.

Bemelmans's letter to Massee of 2 May 1961 shows both the extent to which he believed in the importance of letting the image carry the story and the extent to which he was willing to defer to her leadership. For instance, apparently basing her comments on a reading of the text in isolation from the illustrations, Massee was concerned that four-year-olds might not be able to follow the jump from the place where, in the final version, Miss Clavel says, "Quick, darlings, pack your bags, and we'll get / Out to the airport and catch the next jet" (*ML,* 9), and the next segment that reads, "Fill the house with lovely flowers, / Fly our flags from all the towers" (*ML,* 10). Bemelmans agreed that four-year-olds would need the help of adults in some instances, but "four year olds get older, and the rest of the readrs [*sic*] ae [*sic*] older to start with otherwise we wouldn't have such a large edition."[57] Arguing for the predominance of the image as storyteller, he advanced that "in the first Madeline, the picture of the man hobbling across the Invalides with the words: And sometimes they were very sad—would have to have been supported by the explanation in rhyme, that this was a military hospital, supported and created by Napoleon, for the invalided soldiers of the campaigns of Austerlitz etc." Nevertheless, "since you are who you are," and appreciating Massee's need to "face the librarians," Bemelmans agreed to cooperate if she still insisted after reading with pictures and text adjacent, and if she would tell him exactly which verbal explanations she thought were necessary. Nevertheless, he notes, "I do that reluctantly, for it slows speeds, [*sic*] it is in my understanding of the childs [*sic*] mind of no import, for he is concerned to get to the story and the story seems to me eminently simple." It would seem that Bemelmans prevailed in the instance of the page turn between Paris and London, for only the image—not the text—clarifies that the place and speakers have changed.

Apparently, Massee's comments caused Bemelmans to do a kind of field research in London with a group of young children before the book was finalized. In doing so, he realized the omission of a picture essential to the story line: "The terrible blow came—and deservedly so when a little girl asked—Where is the horse eating the apples and roses—? Since the essence of prasnce [presence?] is to show —rather than talk that is a great fault . . . which I should have caught."[58] Bemelmans included a sketch of the horse in the garden and offered to fly to New York to fix the picture, so intent was he on the importance of this addition. The final book includes a full-page picture of the horse devouring the garden at night; it perfectly sets the stage for the sunny full-page picture on the right-hand side in which the gardener starts out the door to where disaster awaits him (*ML,* 40–41).

Bemelmans and his editors struggled for a long time with the verses for *Madeline in London,* trying to get rhythm, rhyme, and meaning ironed out. Additionally, in mid-May, Bemelmans sent Massee some lines rewritten by *Holiday* magazine editors that he preferred to his own, letting Viking make the final decision on these.[59] Pictures and text were completed by mid-June 1961, and on 7 July Bemelmans expressed to a Viking editor "my deep thanks to you and everyone—I am sure we have a joyful book and something good for the kids and the parents."[60] The statement suggests both his commitment to quality and his certainty that adults as well as children would enjoy this book.

Madeline in London was a Junior Literary Guild selection, as a number of Bemelmans's books had been, an honor that in itself increased sales. With his typical flair for publicity, Bemelmans made plans for publicizing the book that included an exhibition, "drum beating," and a luncheon of the 12 little girls and Miss Clavel at the palace (11 October 1960). He later requested copies of the book to give to the Queen, noting that "the children at the Palace have them all, and love them."[61]

Unfortunately, the product of so much care, energy, and matured talent was completely overlooked by the Caldecott Committee. In *The Child's First Books: A Critical Study of Pictures and Text,* Donnarae MacCann and Olga Richards suggest that the reason for an omission of this type lies in a selection committee not well qualified to evaluate art.[62] Nevertheless, *Madeline in London* continues to delight children everywhere with its depictions of Madeline, horses, pageantry, and birthday cakes. The plot is jolly and warm, and the full-color illustrations of London are beautiful and authentic. The fact that the book remains in print more than 30 years later suggests that Bemelmans knew what he was about when he wrote that "this is forever" (29 October 1960).

While *Madeline in London* was in its final stages, Bemelmans wrote happily to Massee of thoughts for a new book involving Madeline in Washington, D.C. He had dined at the White House, and both Jackie Kennedy and Caroline were to help with it. He had driven around town and noted "magnificent" scenery.[63] Unfortunately, none of this was ever to come to pass. Bemelmans died a year and half later.

Madeline's Christmas. In 1985 Viking responded to the continuing popularity of the *Madeline* books with the publication of one that

Bemelmans had never finished in the standard Viking format, *Madeline's Christmas*. Thirty years before, in June 1956, while Viking and Bemelmans were hard at work finishing *Madeline and the Bad Hat,* Bemelmans sent May Massee the first draft of this work, which he intended for the upcoming *McCall's* Christmas issue. In a letter of 23 June he asks Massee to give the work her attention, noting that "unfortunately this work did not have the benefit of long reflection," and requesting help in meeting his 1 August deadline if other drawings or changes in color were needed.[64] Enclosing the first draft of the text in a letter of 27 June, he again welcomed Viking's assistance, noting that "time is of the essence."[65] The work appeared five months later in the December issue, as a small self-cover book insert, 24 pages on comic-book—quality paper. This was the second time *McCall's* and Madeline had worked together for mutual benefit at Christmas, the first time having been with the initial appearance of *Madeline's Rescue* in December 1951.

Both the *McCall's* and the Viking version of *Madeline's Christmas* open with the well-known introductory verse and an appealing variation of the "old house" image set in the snow. Everyone in school is sick in bed with a cold, except Madeline, who is caring for all the others. From a mysterious rug merchant-magician who appears at the door, she purchases foot rugs for everyone's "ice-cold-in-the-morning feet."[66] (The Viking version reads "ice-cold in the morning feet."[67]) When the rug merchant reappears, nearly frozen without his rugs, she invites him in, thaws him out, and lets him help her with the dishes. While Madeline goes out for a Christmas tree, the magician says magic words that send all 12 little girls sailing on carpets to their own homes for Christmas. But when Miss Clavel rings her school bell, they fly back home, and, on the final page, sit at the table and wave greetings to the reader.

Both the *McCall's* version of *Madeline's Christmas* and the 1985 Viking version differ from the standard *Madeline* books in a number of ways. First of all, the story is about half as long as the others, and the plot is undeveloped. The magician's appearance from nowhere is a bit abrupt, and the climax is a piece of Christmas gaiety that satisfies the heart of every reader who has ever longed to see the little girls reunited with their parents but that solves no problem clearly presented in the book. Because the *McCall's* book has a self-cover, the 1985 version lacks the endpapers that so strikingly introduce the other works. All of the pages are in full color; none is in the typical yellow wash. Inasmuch as most of the action takes place inside the old house, the illustrations do little to introduce readers to the culture and sites of Paris. Even Madeline herself has a somewhat changed nature. No longer is she both the source of the problem as well as the one with inventive solutions, as she was in the last three books of the series—*Madeline and the Bad Hat, Madeline and the Gypsies,* and *Madeline in London;* instead she is all solution, busily helping the others, even Miss Clavel.

In the second letter to Massee, Bemelmans quickly outlined an introduction for an expanded Viking version. After the standard opening, the little girls would walk around Paris "in the four seasons" (27 June 1956). They see a rug merchant who "is selling rugs to atone for a bad thing he did until he does a good thing and regains his magic powers." They catch cold either in the rain or because the Bad Hat overturns their boat. Such an introduction would have given Bemelmans the chance both to include scenes of Paris and to create the magician's motivation for magically whisking the girls home—that is, this would be the "good thing" he needs to do.

Bemelmans never completed the expansion of *Madeline's Christmas,* however. The spring of 1957 saw the publication of *Madeline and the Bad Hat;* as a marketing strategy, he liked to space out the appearance of the *Madeline* books, letting each one take hold (23 June 1956). After two more *Madeline* books, he returned to *Madeline's Christmas* in 1962, planning to call the expanded version *Madeline and the Magician.* Sadly, however, his death on 2 October prevented his completion of the work. In a letter to Massee dated 20 July 1962, he had anticipated a 1964 publication, in order to have time to "go through all the agonies that these books require before they are perfect"[68]—agonies that he had experienced only the year before with *Madeline in London.* With typical enthusiasm, as he contemplated *Madeline and the Magician,* he noted that "this is now in my mind, the richest and most gay of all the books, [*sic*] it has besides Mustapha, the rug selling Magician also Christmas in it and I have the very framework for it done."

Despite the embryonic state, then, of the *McCall's Madeline's Christmas,* Viking decided to reissue the work in 1985. The book depended for its appeal not only on its own relatively slim merits, but above all on the delight of fans everywhere—and of all ages—at a new addition to the *Madeline* corpus. Inasmuch as only a few pieces of the original art were still available, many of them having apparently been sold at a December 1956 Hammer Galleries exhibit,[69] to restore the illustrations was Viking's first challenge. In the absence of Bemelmans's originals, Viking's Jody Wheeler worked from the diminutive 1956 publication (13 cm by 18.5 cm), photographically enlarging and recoloring. A slight alteration was also made—a hanging lamp that blocked the head of the magician in the original kitchen scene was removed. Visually, the 1985 edition is a faithful enhancement of the 1956 version: the colors are brighter, and the images cleaner on the larger, smoother paper.

The 1985 edition presents other changes as well. For it, the original version was redesigned, with pictures and words arranged somewhat differently. The opening was expanded by two pictures, seemingly created by making slight changes to other Bemelmans illustrations. On the second page of text, snow has been added to the scene of "the tiger in the zoo" first presented in *Madeline;* and an introductory dormitory scene has been inserted, seemingly created by removing Madeline and the magician from one that appears later. Besides adding illustrations, the Viking version also changes the *McCall's* original by eliminating two pictures: one of the magician outside in a square of Paris, and one of Miss Clavel ringing the bell to call the girls back to school after their visits home. In the second case, a bell has been added to Miss Clavel's hand in the next picture, thereby communicating the same information.

Finally, many lines of verse have been changed, either to make them scan more perfectly or to eliminate concepts or words that Viking editors in 1985 apparently judged confusing for young readers. For instance, below the picture of Madeline on the front doorstep pouring a kettle of hot water at the feet of the frozen magician, the original reads: "He made it—back to Madeline's at last— / But, poor man, he was frozen fast." The revision eliminates the pun and reads, "He made it—back to Madeline's door— / He couldn't take one footstep more." In the climax written by Bemelmans and his editors some 30 years earlier, the text reads, "So, in Dallas and Rome / And on the Panamanian Isthmus, / The little girls were all home / FOR CHRISTMAS!!!!!"[70] This line, so intriguing both rhythmically and intellectually, has been changed to "And twelve little girls were on their way— / To surprise their parents on Christmas Day." Madeleine Bemelmans has written that "Barbara and I would have preferred the original text for the 1985 *Madeline's Christmas.* The changes were made at the request of Viking Penguin—some of them by the editors of Children's Books, some by me" (letter to author, 31 July 1988).

Maintaining tradition, *McCall's* again published "Madeline's Christmas" in its December 1985 issue, this time in a series of pictures spread across several pages.[71] Although not all of the pictures appear, the verbal text is complete and identical to that of the Viking book.

Early *Madeline* Offshoots

During Bemelmans's lifetime, *Madeline* appeared a number of times in editions other than the standard Viking publications. Two less expensive versions of *Madeline* appeared in 1954, a Little Golden Book *Madeline* in the standard Little Golden Book format,[72] which cost only a quarter (Pomerance, 102) and a one-dollar Goldencraft version of this edition (*Publishers Weekly,* 14 November 1960, 17). One of the most striking changes in the Little Golden Book version, aside from the size, is the use of color on every page. Instead of being displayed against a background of yellow wash, the line drawings are colored; for instance, the little girls' nightgowns and bed sheets are a variety of pastel hues—peach, green, blue, and yellow. Although the line drawings have been reduced to fit on the page, full-color pages have been cropped; thus, their margins and even the original pictures' edges are missing. The result, while communicating the basic story, lacks a number of the illustrations, as well as the pleasing overall design of the original.

Although the *Madeline* books in the original Viking series are the only ones remaining in print, two other *Madeline* books appeared after *Madeline's Rescue* and before the next Viking book, *Madeline and the Bad Hat.* Both of these feature Madeline in Christmas stories. The first was called "Madeline's Christmas" in the December 1955 *Good Housekeeping* version[73] and *Madeline's Christmas in Texas* when Neiman Marcus presented it that year as a paperback publication.[74] The second of these, which appeared as an insert in the December 1956 *McCall's,* was also called *Madeline's Christmas* and was the basis for the 1985 Viking version, already discussed. Both of these Christmas works are considerably shorter and of smaller format than the standard *Madeline* books. Interestingly, in both, Bemelmans suggests biological relatives who are absent in the Viking books, and in the Texas Christmas story he gives Madeline a last name, Fogg (74).

Bemelmans used Madeline's 1955 Christmas appearance as part of a larger Madeline publicity campaign. In both the *Good Housekeeping* version and the Neiman Marcus version, Madeline and her friends fly to Texas to claim an inheritance from her departed oil-and-cattle-rich great-grandfather. In 16 small pages, 17.8 cm by 12.3 cm (wider than tall), the book extols the Christmas wonders of "Neiman-Marcus, / The world's greatest store," where Madeline, having fallen asleep on a camping display cot, is rescued by the Texas Rangers. In the magazine version, Madeline goes to a never-identified department store and, overwhelmed with her anticipated riches, becomes greedy and "haughty" (75). In both versions, Madeline learns to her dismay that she will not receive her inheritance until she is 21, and thus returns to Paris. The magazine version contains only seven illustrations, some of them identical to those used in the book. The book consists of a single signature fold, with two staples, and a slightly stiffer paper for the cover. Although there are some touches of red on the cover, the rest of the book is done not in the typical yellow but in a lavender wash.[75] It seems likely that the book was a department store giveaway, inasmuch as the inside front cover reads, "This book is a christmas [*sic*] gift to you from Neiman-Marcus."

Bemelmans's text and pictures for "Madeline's Christmas" in *Good Housekeeping* are followed by four pages of Madeline fashions and toys available at Neiman Marcus in Dallas and Houston. Beautiful child models display a Madeline cape and hat, nightgown, robe, dress, and playwear, all done in France's national colors—blue, white, and red. A Madeline doll sports a changeable Madeline wardrobe and plays with a Genevieve dog doll. Two of the pages are decorated with Bemelmans's sketches. Although Neiman Marcus is never mentioned by name in the magazine version of the story, clearly the Neiman Marcus book and the magazine version represent a coordinated advertising effort benefiting Bemelmans, Neiman Marcus, and *Good Housekeeping*.

Dressing little girls "à la Madeline" continued to be popular in Bemelmans's lifetime. Several years after the 1955 *Good Housekeeping/ Neiman Marcus* spread, a Rochester, New York, paper declared the Madeline look to be the favorite for the season, and showed little girls in large-brimmed Breton rollers made of straw with colored streamers.[76]

During Bemelmans's lifetime there appeared a number of films and filmstrips based on the Madeline books. In 1960 an hour-long adaptation of the stories aired on the *Shirley Temple Show* (*Publishers Weekly,* 14 November 1960, 16).

Of the many books published, only a few become classics. In *Madeline* Bemelmans created a book that appealed on many levels to adults as well as to children. Knowing this, he built on his original success with energy and ingenuity for the last 12 years of his life. In her article on Bemelmans, Ethel Heins points to the "commercialism rampant in the present-day world of children's books" (Heins, 55), a commercialism of which Bemelmans himself was the artful master several decades ago. Each new format change, gallery showing, publicity event, and media presentation both drew upon and enhanced the popularity of the books.

While the effect of Bemelmans's skillful marketing on the longevity of the series cannot be overemphasized, other factors intrinsic to the works contribute equally to their contemporary success. The *Madeline* books are beautiful, funny, and surprisingly modern, in ways I will examine in chapter 5.

Chapter Four
Children's Books for Adults

During the 1940s, 1950s, and early 1960s, in addition to *Madeline*'s many sequels, Bemelmans continued to produce other books that were marketed to a juvenile audience. Like most of the *Madeline* series, most of these books appeared in adult magazines as well as in hardcover. Yet none of these books was ever as successful in addressing both audiences as the *Madeline* books were; in fact, most of them display a certain disregard for the young reader, ignoring wholly or in part traditional norms of children's literature. Most lack a child protagonist. In some, Bemelmans seems unconcerned about the value of the lesson he imparts. In others, the experiences, language, and sources of humor seem more appropriate for adults than for children.

Fifi

In 1940, about a year after *Madeline,* Simon & Schuster published *Fifi,* named after a French poodle who lives a coddled existence in Uganda, the spoiled pet of Lord and Lady Fimple Fample. Like the poodle of Count Hungerburg von Hungerburg before her, Fifi has the habit of chasing cats: "Twice a day she chased the cat / up and down a coco-mat."[1] On a stopover during a plane trip across Africa to visit Lady Fample's dentist in Zanzibar, Fifi runs after what she believes to be a cat, only to find herself face to face with a leopard. A native rescues her from the leopard and takes her home to his wife for dinner. Staring at her captors and the alligator-infested river that separates her from freedom, Fifi tearfully promises never to chase a cat again. "An old secretary bird" cynically admonishes, "Ashes to ashes / and dust to dust / if the lions / don't get you / the pythons must." Just as the bird wishes her good-bye, Lady Fample rescues Fifi from the jungle, tromping in and offering the natives "some rings for your noses— / which I always carry for such purposes." With Fifi under her arm, she marches to her waiting plane and flies on to keep her appointment with Dr. Gay. At first glance *Fifi* recalls *Madeline,* upon the success of which Simon & Schuster was doubtless trying to capitalize.

The large format resembles that of its famous predecessor, as does the illustration on the first page, a substantial, elegant, and essentially symmetrical house, home of the Famples. Again, as in *Madeline,* Bemelmans narrates his story in quirky rhymed couplets. And his title character is a beguiling and saucy French female who wears a hair ribbon and has to be rescued by adults.

Despite its name, however, *Fifi* is not focused uniquely on the mishaps of the poodle. The caricature of the silly and overbearing Lady Fample provides an equally important focus, and one directed primarily to the sophisticated adult reader, who could have enjoyed the story in *Town and Country,* where it appeared the same year.[2] Furthermore, this caricature comes into direct conflict with any moral that the child reader might learn, for Fifi's need for correction is not established early enough in the story to be seen as the conflict. Unlike Peter Rabbit's mother, who warns her mischievous boy not to enter Mr. McGregor's garden at the book's outset, the pampering Lady Fample ignores Fifi's naughtiness— if the reader is to regard it as such—without even scolding her. In one four-cartoon sequence, Fifi runs after a cat at the travel bureau and finally stands slobbering on the desk, without attracting so much as a turn of the head from Lady Fample. True, as she is about to die, Fifi promises "I never, never, NEVER will chase another cat." But any lesson of obedience that the child reader might absorb is confused by this indulgent "parenting."

Like Madeline, Fifi needs rescuing; unlike Madeline, however, she is clearly not a "child" character—she even has a boyfriend, a large comfortable-looking springer spaniel. (In the magazine version, this dog is another French poodle.) Furthermore, she lacks the relatively austere and parentless existence that makes Madeline at once so brave and so touching, instead living a spoiled life much like that of her mistress, Lady Fample. Every day after chasing the cat, "she looked everywhere/to see if the ribbon in her hair / was still there. / Fifi also had a beau / whom everyone was proud to know." On the book's front cover, Fifi sits regally in an armchair, while the other dog stands worshipfully alongside.

Fifi's pointy hair ribbon and sculpted French poodle head and tail provide ready marks of visual identification. The bow stands out all the more in that it provides almost the only touch of red in the book's brown/green color scheme. Signalling his poodle-heroine's coddled existence, on the opening page, Bemelmans depicts Lady Fample tying the saucy bow in place on her pet's fluffy white head. In one hypothetical sequence, a long green python devours Fifi. The red hair bow lies nearby, suggesting a dangerous loss of identity; yet the outline of her fluffy head and tail in the snake comically suggests that Fifi can still be restored intact. After Fifi's ordeal, Lady Fample restores her to normalcy with "a new ribbon for your hair." Throughout the book the shape of the ribbon itself acts as a barometer to Fifi's mood; its perky corners droop alarmingly over her ears when the native first picks her up by the head, and point tensely in the direction of the alligator-infested river while Fifi "started to shiver."

For the most part, *Fifi* is visually disappointing. The book's brown and green cartoons lack the energy of *Madeline*'s yellow washes, and Bemelman's double-page spreads of repeated patterns of animals are of uneven interest. The striking red, white, and black endpapers, however, wittily establish an important subject of the book to come, with an overall Escher-like design of poodles endlessly chasing cats running from poodles. In *Fifi,* as in *Hansi, The Castle Number Nine,* and *Noodle,* Bemelmans's drawings deftly reveal his special sensitivity to the postures and moods of dogs.

Clearly, in *Fifi* Bemelmans has moved away from the impetus of his first books to teach young readers about life in a real foreign country. Even though the book is set in Africa, this is an Africa of 1940s stereotypes—of lions, pythons, and, most regrettably, of primitive and foolish savages. The man who captures Fifi looks at once childlike and wild wearing Fifi's red bow in his hair and holding a knife between his teeth. The accompanying childish phrasing enhances a sense of his immaturity: "And the native made bum-bum / on his ceremonial drum." Later, he looks as surprised and sullen as a disappointed baby when Lady Fample takes Fifi from him. Her words are condescending: "Here are some rings for your noses— / which I always carry for such purposes." The native's large nose, gigantic lips, and wide white eyes recall those of a minstrel show singer.

Bemelmans does not focus for long on Fifi's captors. They are basically there to enhance his caricature of Lady Fample, a formidable woman so strong-willed and silly about her French poodle that she will walk through pythons, tigers, and unfriendly natives to rescue her. Fortunately, such insulting stereotypes, no matter how incidental, no longer have a place in publishing. This reason alone would suffice to keep *Fifi* out of print.

Rosebud

According to Bemelmans, he based his next children's book, *Rosebud*, on an African folk tale.[3] A rabbit outwitting larger antagonists brought Brer Rabbit to the mind of at least one critic.[4] The story, under the title of "Nosegay," was published in the April 1942 issue of *Town and Country*.[5] Random House brought out *Rosebud* later that fall. This is the first book that Bemelmans both wrote and illustrated in which there are no human beings, only talking creatures. Despite this nod in the direction of a typical children's genre, the work fails either to teach or to entertain.

The plot of *Rosebud*, like that of Munro Leaf's *Noodle*, is structured by the device of doing something first to one character and then to another. The rabbit protagonist, Rosebud, is "very happy" (*R, 3*) until he reads a book that praises the sterling qualities of large animals such as the elephant and the whale, while describing the rabbit as a "small rodent who . . . is scared, shy and hysterical" (*R, 9*). A sudden noise draws Rosebud's attention to a whale; remembering the book, he overcomes his first sense of fear and challenges the whale to a rope-pulling contest that night. Next Rosebud goes into the jungle and taunts an elephant, likewise challenging him to a tug-of-war. Later, in the moonlight, Rosebud ties the whale and the elephant to each other without their realizing it. The two giants pull and pull until the rope snaps; the elephant lands on his back, "while the Whale came to grief on a coral reef" (*R, 29*). Rosebud mocks each in turn, concluding, "Remember forever that one must never make fun of little people" (*R, 31*). Afterwards, Rosebud begins writing a "magnificent book about the strength and smartness and the great courage of rabbits" (*R, 32*).

Madeleine Bemelmans has suggested that "the name 'Rosebud' may have occurred to Ludwig after he saw the Orson Welles film *Citizen Kane*."[6] "Rosebud," Kane's dying word, resonates throughout this movie, which had come out only the year before, in 1941. Perhaps, then, Bemelmans changed the magazine title from "Nosegay" to "Rosebud" partly because he thought the word alone would attract curiosity and sales. Perhaps the name also suggested color possibilities for the book: in a letter to Massee in June 1941 he mentions "a lovely soft rosy baby pink."[7] Finally, he may have enjoyed the irony of attaching this gentle, soft-sounding name to his grumpy yet determined hero.

Viewed as a fable, *Rosebud* fails primarily because the story provides no adequate reason for Rosebud's attack on this particular whale or elephant. They are not making "fun of little people"; they just happen to be there as objects of his frustration. True, the whale "laughed so loud that the sea was filled with ripples" (*R*, 14) after accepting Rosebud's challenge; however, neither Bemelmans's text nor illustrations clarifies whether this laughter suggests derision or, in fact, goodwill. In the absence of a clear villain, Rosebud seems merely to be an insecure sort who feels good about winning an unfair fight with a reluctant opponent.

Viewed not as a moral tale but as ironic humor, *Rosebud* falls short also for lack of a consistent authorial perspective. On the one hand, the ironic contradiction between the character's disposition and his name is striking. The front cover depicts Rosebud with a typical scowl; his crossed arms and crossed ears repeat the basic image of the cross-patterned, almost "thorny" frame. The endpapers depict rabbits shooting guns and lifting barbells. On the other hand, the final lines of the story, in which Rosebud writes a "magnificent book about the strength and smartness and the great courage of rabbits," are not so clearly ironic; for although Rosebud has not demonstrated "strength," he has nevertheless displayed a kind of "courage" and "smartness" in approaching and tricking animals larger than he is.

Not even the playful, inventive illustrations of *Rosebud* can compensate for an unlovable character and a confusing authorial tone. Visually, Rosebud himself is the typical Bemelmans rabbit—long-bodied, long-legged, walking upright like those on the endpapers of *The Castle Number Nine*. As in *Noodle*, Bemelmans matches a spare cartooning technique to a simple story line: Rosebud, the whale, and the elephant are depicted through flat, smoothly outlined shapes with a minimum of carefully chosen detail to suggest facial expression or activity. The work's pink, blue, and purple color scheme lightens its mood, the pink being in harmony with Rosebud's name, if not his character. Around some illustrations Bemelmans creates whimsical frames and, with similar whimsy, leaves others unframed.

The magazine version of this story is marginally superior. The text is rhymed, giving the lines more snap; one of the few that found its way into the book with a minor alteration is the above cited "the poor whale came to grief on the edge of a coral reef" (42). Furthermore, the whale's retort to Nosegay's challenge establishes an evil intent, thereby making his defeat desirable: "I will take the rope and grab it, and that will be the end of rabbit" (43).

In a letter to Massee of 20 June 1941, Bemelmans mentions that in a hurried visit to New York, he had had no chance to find out if she liked

Rosebud or not, but that he had taken "the liberty" of discussing layout with Viking's Milton Glick. In a reference to two of Munro Leaf's books, he mentions that "upright, like Ferdinand, might be better, than sideways like Noodle." Perhaps Massee rejected this book as inferior stuff for young readers; in any event, Random House, not Viking, published it.

In 1993 Alfred A. Knopf reprinted *Rosebud* as part of its Umbrella Book collection with one striking change: Rosebud no longer scowls on the front cover as he does in the original edition. Instead, he is leaning back, relaxed and smiling, just as he appears on the first page before he has read the insulting tome. Simply by changing the reader's initial image of Rosebud, the new edition takes on a much cheerier tone. The book is visually brighter also, with a whiter paper and somewhat brighter shades of pink and blue. The text is unchanged, although the print is slightly larger and easier on the eyes. Nevertheless, despite these changes, the book is far from Bemelmans at his wittiest or most charming.

A Tale of Two Glimps

Bemelmans's next book with cartooned characters, *A Tale of Two Glimps,* may not even have been intended for children. Although it was included in R. R. Bowker's *Fiction, Folklore, Fantasy, and Poetry for Children, 1876–1985* in 1986,[8] no reviews appeared in major newspapers or magazines at the time of its 1947 publication. Published by the Columbia Broadcasting System and distributed to CBS associates without charge (Pomerance, 171), the work's primary focus is on the superior virtues of color television. In fact, the book bears a dedication "to the young in heart," whose "vision . . . has given us the miracle of television,"[9] presumably those dreamers and engineers who created what has since become such a pervasive medium. Bemelmans, imaginative and well connected, would quickly learn to employ the potential of television to enhance his own projects.

For the child reader, *A Tale of Two Glimps* offers very little aside from funny-looking characters and bright colors. On the other hand, for an adult it is a visually witty romp, "much ado about nothing." The "glimps" are fantastic creatures—somewhat human/donkeylike in appearance—named for their primary activity, "glimpsing" television. The black-and-white glimp lives in a gray room, watching a black-and-white television. The other glimp, "a lovely shade of orange," lives in a highly colorful room and watches a color TV. Images of first a pastry chef and then a dance team on his TV sadden and bore the black-and-white glimp, while the same programs stimulate and interest the orange glimp. Finally, after realizing that his TV has misled him into thinking that "Greenville" rather than "Orangeville" has won the football game, the black-and-white glimp can stand it no more. He decides to paint everything in his house; "he even painted himself." But when he can't paint his color TV, "because black-and-white sets just won't receive pictures in color," he marries the colored glimp, and they live happily together with "everything in color . . . even their television pictures . . . and that's why you see them smiling all the time."

Whatever market the book may have originally targeted, *A Tale of Two Glimps* is not particularly suited to children. The glimps are adults, not children, whose primary activity, both before and after marrying, is to watch television. Clearly, a story with an elaborately drawn "moral" that culminates in a blissful marriage draws on children's story traditions; yet the trivial message—the superiority of color TV—and the suggestion that adults should marry in order to acquire a different television set uses such conventions ironically, creating a book that amuses an adult but might bore or mislead a child.

Bemelmans's use of many bright colors lends a spirit of gaiety to this work. As he does in so many other works, he forecasts the entire action of the story on the front cover and the title page. On the left side of the front cover, a frowning black-and-white glimp courts a disapproving colored glimp on the right. Then, two pages later, on the title page, the glimps, now both colored, unite in the center in a smiling embrace. As the story progresses, parallel illustrations with the black-and-white scene always on the left-hand side of a double-page spread and the colored on the right effectively underscore the dullness and confusing aspects of the black-and-white TV screen. The illustrations convey the same message as the text: add color and voilà! how much more clearly we understand, how much happier we feel! Viewed from outside his window, the black-and-white glimp provides a startling contrast to the colorful flowers and butterflies in his garden. How could such a creature exist? the story seems to ask. Color is vastly more natural! Just as Bemelmans plays with the conventions of representation in *Madeline,* so, too, does he here, underscoring the arbitrary and illusory nature of art by coloring one-half of a scene and not the other. At one point, he even has the black-and-white glimp stretch "his neck way over to the colored glimp's side of the book" to see her TV.

Sunshine: A Story about the City of New York

As described, in the early 1940s Bemelmans presented *Fifi* and *Rosebud* in *Town and Country* magazine and also published them as hardcover books. In a letter to Massee of 1 November 1949, he described the financial benefits of such an arrangement: "write a childrens book [*sic*] let a National Magazine print it first . . . then make a childrens [*sic*] book of greater length out of it, benefit to the publisher, Advertising and free plates."[10] The letter was written from "Aboard the Dolphin in Naples," on stationery listing addresses in New York City; Danbury, Connecticut; Paris; and Lech am Arlberg in Austria. Clearly, Bemelmans saw no reason not to make children's literature as lucrative as possible in order to satisfy "the voracious appetite that feeds my hungry self." Only one month after this letter, he once again set this process in motion by publishing a Christmas story in *Good Housekeeping* entitled "Sunshine, Sunshine, Go Away: A Story about the City of New York" (December 1949). That spring the Simon & Schuster juvenile appeared under the title *Sunshine: A Story about the City of New York*.[11] Although the book is visually successful, it may fail to engage a young reader not because of any minor flaws but because the basic story has more appeal to older readers: the principal characters are adults and the plot hinges on actions somewhat outside of a child's immediate comprehension.

The plot of *Sunshine* is both highly improbable and filled with amusing ironies. In the midst of a housing shortage, a mean New York landlord named Sunshine, after turning away countless applicants, finally decides to let his gloomy Gramercy Park flat to the elderly and seemingly harmless little Miss Moore. After signing a five-year lease, however, Miss Moore opens a music school for children and conducts orchestra rehearsals in the apartment. Unable to sleep and desperate, Sunshine moves. One rainy day, after naively bidding ten cents for an umbrella at an auction, Miss Moore discovers that she has bought not one umbrella, but two thousand umbrellas at ten cents each. This financial blow leaves her unable to pay the rent and thus prey to Sunshine's desire to evict her. But Miss Moore has a plan. Giving a twist to an old saying, she exclaims, "Sunshine, Sunshine, go away / And come again some other day!" Soon the skies open up and "the rain / Came down like out of a water main." Walking through the drenched neighborhoods of New York, Miss Moore and her little music students sell every last umbrella to the soaked New Yorkers, thereby raising the money to save the school. After giving a Christmas concert in snowy Gramercy Park, Miss Moore opens her apartment door to a repentent Sunshine, who begs her to let him come back to the neighborhood. She invites him in, and "The cat sat on his lap and purred with mirth, / The dog lay at his feet, and peace was on earth."

A number of aspects of *Sunshine* appeal more fully to adults than to children. True, its presentation of New York recalls *Madeline*'s didactic approach: large, full-color pictures, with identifying text, depict various neighborhoods and monuments of the city that is America's answer to Paris. Only the adult reader, however, can fully take pleasure in the irony of "a story about New York" in which a little old lady outwits a grouchy landlord in the midst of a housing shortage. In fact, too much of the subject matter—leases, tenants, auctions, and lawyers—is outside of the realm of a child's immediate knowledge, a point that reviewers were quick to point out.[12]

On the level of caricature, too, only the adult can fully realize the text's meanings. This is not to say that the young reader can find no sympathetic character. No doubt a child will take pleasure in Miss Moore herself, inasmuch as she is often surrounded by happy children. A child will understand that there is a conflict between a scowling, fist-raising man and a white-haired old lady so kind that she brushes snow off the sidewalk to permit the birds to eat. Yet the more subtle aspects of the caricature will escape a child reader, as for instance, when Sunshine says at the end, "And the thing that mostly grates me— / Is that my own lawyer hates me."

As noted, Bemelmans wondered in a letter to Massee if *The Castle Number Nine* (1937) hadn't sold better "because there are no children in it" (1 November 1949). A comparison of the magazine and the book versions of *Sunshine* reveals several ways in which Bemelmans shaped what is essentially a conflict between adults as to make children more prominent in the juvenile publication. For instance, his introductory illustrations differ. At the outset of the magazine version there appears a large, long-distance perspective of people of all sizes ice skating at Rockefeller Center (63). For the front cover of the picturebook, however, Bemelmans uses an illustration (taken from elsewhere in the magazine version) in which a child in a bright yellow slicker is centered in the foreground, probably on the deck of the Staten Island Ferry, selling umbrellas to storm-soaked passengers.

In some instances, Bemelmans's revisions of the magazine version in order to appeal to a young audience produced awkward results. For instance, he alters the sequence of pictures in which Miss Moore and the

children deliver umbrellas around New York. In the magazine version—
the version more obviously directed to adults—an adult, Miss Moore,
takes the lead in her own rescue scheme: "Miss Moore ascended the
Heights / And sold umbrellas to Brooklynites" (74). The picturebook
version moves the illustration of Miss Moore selling umbrellas to *fourth*
place after three pages showing *children* selling umbrellas. Thus the
book's sequence begins with the action of a child: "Rusty Regan took
pity / On the Mayor's reception committee." The illustration shows a
boy handing an umbrella to a man in a top hat. Unfortunately, although
shuffling pictures around in this manner effectively permits Bemelmans
to appeal to his young readers' sense of heroism, the book version is
momentarily confusing at this point for two reasons. First of all, none of
the other children is presented by name; consequently the reader is
caught off guard at first, wondering if Rusty Regan is the child in the
midst of a fairly large group of adults, or if he is one of the adults, perhaps the smiling man in the center. Second, the meaning of the phrase
"took pity on the Mayor's reception committee" is unclear until selling
umbrellas has been established as the essential action, to which "taking
pity"—namely giving them away—reflects a kind of exception.

Turning a Christmas story for adults into a book for children to be
published sometime after Christmas resulted in vagueness in the book's
setting. The first requirement no doubt inspired Bemelmans to turn to
Dickens for a Scrooge-like character on whom the season works its
magic. Aside from the endpapers, however, where the conclusion is subtly forecast by a picture of a small child carrying an undecorated ever-
green tree alongside snowy New York harbor, Christmas is entirely
absent in the book's illustrations and text until the final scenes.
Furthermore, except for two snowy illustrations near the outset, the pictures do not even suggest that it is winter. After that, 29 pages pass that
show either indoor scenes or outdoor pictures of either sunshine or rain,
but never snow. Thus the page turn near the end that takes the reader
from an indoor concert at Carnegie Hall to a snowy scene of Christmas
caroling in Gramercy Park advances time too abruptly.

The book, published by Simon & Schuster, has the same large format
as Bemelmans's two preceding Simon and Schuster publications,
Madeline and *Fifi*. The cover bears a particular resemblance to that of
Madeline, with a full-color image on the front and a sketch in black ink
on yellow on the back. Inside, the full-color cityscapes recall the Paris
settings of *Madeline* in their expressionistic use of wash and calligraphic
line. On the two-color pages Bemelmans alternates between yellow,

lavender, and pale red wash rather than using yellow wash consistently, as he had done in *Madeline.* The sun, Bemelmans's icon for warmth and cheer so prevalent in *Madeline* and *Quito Express,* appears also in *Sunshine.* The very title of this work, even though used ironically as the name of the crabby landlord, suggests Bemelmans's special feeling for this golden element of nature.

Sunshine offers much of what is best in Bemelmans's picturebooks: large picture surfaces filled with interesting details, a bouncy rhymed text, color, and the didactic value of learning something about a particular place. For all of these reasons, and because the work's energetic and beautiful illustrations gave their own city back to New Yorkers with a humorous treatment of the difficulties of living there, the *New York Herald Tribune* awarded the work its Spring Book Festival Award in the year of its publication, 1950. Despite the extent to which the book repeats some of the features of *Madeline,* however, the adult subject matter and the absence of a child protagonist make this book a much inferior product to the earlier Simon & Schuster publication.

The Happy Place

One year after the critical success of *Sunshine: A Story about the City of New York,* Bemelmans presented *The Happy Place,* a rabbit fantasy set in Central Park, as a seasonal offering in the April 1951 issue of *Woman's Home Companion.*[13] The following year the story appeared in hardcover, with the text complete and virtually unchanged.[14] Bemelmans's only children's work to be published by Little, Brown, the book has a much smaller format than any of his previous works, higher than wide, and is an illustrated text, rather than a picturebook. Illustrations are primarily black pen-and-ink sketches, with three double-page spreads and two large pictures in full color.

The protagonist of this rambling, objectless picaresque, a rabbit named Winthrop, is bought in Bunnyland as an Easter gift for two children who love him nearly to death before the father releases him in Central Park. After a mad dash with a whippet at his heels, Winthrop's only recourse is to leap into a pond, from which he is rescued by a father and son frog. While the three talk, a cormorant dives down, seizes the son from a lily pad, flings him in the air, and catches him in his gullet. The saddened father frog advises Winthrop to leave and find protection and food in the zoo by hitching a ride in the shopping cart of an old German couple who pass by the pond each day on their way there. Once at the zoo, Winthrop befriends a lonely elephant—"a great Viennese waltzer" (*HP*, 41) who needs a dancing partner. Kindly, he does the elephant the favor of retrieving from the zoo director's desk a favorite possession—a glass frog, the gift a little girl had handed through the elephant's cage many years before. Delighted, the elephant insists that Winthrop take the glass frog to the grieving father frog. The latter has barely set the replica on a lily pad in order to look at it when, once again, the cormorant swoops down. Upon ingesting the figurine, the bird dies quickly, with a convulsive jerking of his legs and wings. All the frogs now come out of hiding, and the pond is once more a "happy place" (*HP*, 31), alive with singing. Winthrop, the wiser for his experiences, observes that "The only thing worth while in this world is to make other people happy" (*HP*, 58). He urges the frog to help him find someone for the lonely elephant to waltz with.

The book conforms to some extent to the fable genre, with talking animal characters and a clearly stated moral at the end. Yet *The Happy Place* moves beyond the fable in the length and complexity of its action and in the reflective, almost philosophical nature of its animal characters. The father frog, the voice of wisdom, describes his son as "an incurable optimist" (*HP*, 26) and observes that "life is precarious" (*HP*, 27) just moments before the cormorant's attack. Like E. B. White's *Charlotte's Web* (1952), another "talking animal" story published in the post–World War II era, *The Happy Place* acknowledges evil and emphasizes the humanitarian value of helping others. The dénouement suggests the possibility of surviving and rebuilding, as so many human beings had done in the previous decades. With its emphasis on mutual assistance and its many touches of humor, *The Happy Place* exemplifies a Bemelmans credo reported at just about the same time as the book's publication. In a *Time* magazine review for 31 March 1952 of an exhibit of some of his paintings, Bemelmans noted that "the purpose of art . . . is to console and amuse—myself, and I hope, others" ("People Watcher," 74).

The story appeals most strongly to the child reader through its situations and characterizations, both of which are enhanced by Bemelmans's illustrations. Winthrop, like Rosebud before him, is a long-bodied animal who walks and holds himself like a human being. Leaning back with his legs crossed, Winthrop appreciatively describes the elephant's waltz as "very elegant" (*HP*, 41). Winthrop peers over his shoulder as he steals by moonlight into the zoo director's office. Making his way back to the pond, he struts in the Police Athletic League Parade with chest held high.

Originally appearing in *Woman's Home Companion, The Happy Place* is another of Bemelmans's children's book not uniquely aimed at young readers. Adults can more fully respond to the work's wit, irony, and caricatures. Displaying his cultivated knowledge of foods, Bemelmans describes Winthrop's Easter feast: "chopped chicken liver, followed by mushroom-barley soup, creamed spinach, cauliflower with butter sauce, and for dessert . . . rum cake, baked apple and chocolate ice cream" (*HP,* 5). In a combination of German and English words, a stout German couple discuss recipes for *hasenpfeffer*—rabbit stew—while an aghast Winthrop listens on. With the caricature of the sister and brother brat pulling Winthrop in two directions, Bemelmans reminds parents to be responsible bunny buyers.

Bemelmans's placement of opening pictures in the magazine and book versions suggests his awareness of varying audience preferences. Most prominent on the opening spread of *Woman's Home Companion* is the humorous sight of a fat lady sophisticate whose horse has dumped her unceremoniously on her bottom after colliding with Winthrop in Central Park. In the book, however, one of the few pictures in which a child appears—the little girl handing the glass frog to the lonesome elephant—is placed opposite the title page.

One of the few acknowledgments of a child's sensitivities that occurs in the book is the elimination of the phrase "the voracious killer," which is used to describe the cormorant in the magazine version ("The bird of prey, the voracious killer, the cormorant, was still underwater" [*Woman's Home Companion,* 84; *HP,* 27].) Presumably this change was made to bring the book more into line with the prevailing wisdom that children's books should skirt violence. On the other hand, the very presence of a scene in which a young frog is killed while his father watches suggests Bemelmans's unwillingness to concern himself much with this norm. Bemelmans's treatment of the young frog's death suggests that the conflicting demands of writing for both adults and children resulted in a scene not totally satisfactory for either audience. For his younger readers, Bemelmans visually softens the beginning of the attack with a full-color double-page spread showing the frog hanging somewhat comically from the cormorant's mouth (*HP,* 28–29; the picture does not appear at all in the magazine). Furthermore, in nearly identical magazine and hardcover versions, the text has barely introduced the young frog before he is swooped up; thus the reader has no time to become emotionally involved with the character. Finally, the death is described in words which elaborate on the bird's skill while minimizing the frog's response: "He had the unfortunate frog sideways in his beak, threw him up into the air and with deadly accuracy caught him again so that he disappeared down the bird's gullet headfirst" (*Woman's Home Companion,* 84; *HP,* 27, 30). These same techniques that soften the blow for a child contribute to making the death curiously unmoving to an adult. From then on it is remembered as a fact, rather than felt as a loss.

For the most part, *The Happy Place* is easily forgotten. Its moral seems forced: inasmuch as Winthrop was not clearly searching for life's meaning, the philosophical resolution—"The only thing worth while in this world is to make other people happy" (*HP,* 58)—arrives out of nowhere. The plot offers no build-up or suspense, with the cormorant's death a fortunate accident rather than an anticipated climax. On the other hand, the caricatures are deftly drawn, and the title page in which the little girl befriends the elephant provides a nice touch of nostalgia; for that was in 1875 when the elephant was young, and the Victorian era zoogoers wore top hats and carried muffs.

The High World

In *Holiday* magazine for December 1950, only a year after his *Good Housekeeping* presentation "Sunshine, Sunshine, Go Away," Bemelmans presented another seasonal story, "Christmas in Tyrol." Four years were to pass, however, before Harper & Brothers published the book version, entitled *The High World,* in the same year that *Madeline's Rescue* (Viking) won the Caldecott.[15] Within the next seven years, several editions of the work appeared, two of them German (Pomerance, 67–70).

A relatively long, illustrated text, *The High World* is one of Bemelmans's better works for juvenile readers. In more than 100 pages, the author relates his story in a graceful, unhurried prose in perfect harmony with the peaceful setting. As he did in *Hansi,* Bemelmans communicates his intense love for the beauty of the Tyrolean mountains and his admiration for the humor, courage, skill, and kindness of the people of the region. While romanticizing the good folk of Lech, Bemelmans caricatures Austrian officialdom in the person of Dr. Julius Stickle, a government minister who has invaded the peace of the area in order to supervise the construction of a hydroelectric dam financed through the Marshall Plan.

The High World is well constructed, with mounting action and an exciting climax. Early in the story Bemelmans describes fully the amazing power and destructiveness of an avalanche, thereby foreshadowing

the ending. Moving over the course of three Christmases, the story introduces its first complication on a Christmas Eve as Dr. Stickle—the
embodiment of all that is haughty and heartless—arrives at the Old Post
in Lech just in time to spoil the annual celebration of the innkeepers
with their relatives, hunter Tobias Amrainer and his family. Young
Christopher kicks Herr Oberministerialrat in the shin with his hobnail
boot during a tussle over the official's fur hat. The official's wrath soon
grows into a determination to clamp down on Tobias for poaching up in
"the high world" (*HW,* 49, 50), a practice that the needy hunter has
heretofore conducted under the law's tolerant eye. The attempts by the
village *gendarme* to catch Tobias end in comedy, and the Amrainers spend
the second Christmas high on the mountain.

The next spring, Dr. Stickle visits Frau Amrainer to inform her that
the cable car carrying cement to the top of the mountain will pass
directly over their hut. Soon after, the Amrainers insult the official and
find themselves called to court. While the Amrainers are below in Lech,
the experienced mountain dwellers recognize the signs of an impending
avalanche and determine that it will pass directly through the hut where
the five Amrainer children have remained behind. "It was then, suddenly
that the miracle happened. The official became human" (*HW,* 85).
Racing to the controls of the cable car, he lifts five skilled skiers to a
point where they can drop into the deep snow, climb their way out, and
rescue the children. The youngsters are skiied to safety moments before
the avalanche destroys the cable car. The next day the village solves the
poaching problem by giving Tobias the respectable position of forest
ranger. A third Christmas is celebrated with "glow wine," and soon after
the reformed official sponsors the first annual children's ski race.

Only the year before, in *Father, Dear Father,* Bemelmans had reported
his teenage daughter Barbara's objections to the fact that "you fall in
love with your characters and they all turn mushy and nobody is really
bad—they're just odd" (*Father,* 92). Bemelmans, who admitted that he
found it "hard to hate anybody, and impossible to hate anybody for
long" (92), creates the same kind of "mushy" reformation in Herr
Ministerialrat as he did in Mr. Sunshine before him. In fact, the official
becomes so zealous in his plans to bring beneficial technology to the village that the villagers have to ask him nicely to leave things as they are,
and he becomes bitter for a time: "But then the children saved him"
(*HW,* 112). They are enthusiastic about his plans to offer skis and skiing
lessons and to hold an annual ski race. As Bemelmans expanded and
developed the *Holiday* magazine story for a juvenile market, he focused

more closely on young Christopher, named "Pepperl" in the earlier version, introducing the incident in which first Christopher and then the four other Amrainer children fight with the official on the first Christmas Eve. The magazine article, appearing as it does in a travel magazine, begins with a description of the comfortable Austrian inn, the Old Post. The book, however, begins with a description of the High World, the Amrainers and their hut, and the activities of the children in summer and winter. Particular emphasis is placed on the fun Christopher has digging himself out of the snow as well as on his desire for a pair of skis. The book's conclusion maintains this focus: Christopher wins first place in the skiing contest and a special place in the heart of the official.

Anticipating both the name of the child protagonist and the story's dénouement, three pictures of Saint Christopher, protector of children, appear early in the book. On the jacket a traditional depiction hangs on the wall of the Lech church. Leaning on a staff, the good saint tenderly holds a small child on his shoulder. The same image, outlined in pen and ink, appears on the front of the hardcover. Then, opposite the title page, Bemelmans places a humorous version tailored to the setting of his story. Now the child sitting on the saint's shoulder holds a snowball in one hand, and the saint's staff has been replaced with a long pair of skis.

Most of the illustrations in this chapter book are line drawings, every curve deftly conveying character, action, or information about the Tyrolean setting. Occasionally Bemelmans inserts a full-page or double-page colored picture, inviting the eye to examine the many details of a cheerful Tyrolean Christmas or to experience a quiet interior aglow with firelight on wood. Of special note in the work are the seven pages of textless illustrations that convey the excitement of the children's descent to safety.

Several aspects of *The High World* have their basis in reality. The book jacket states that the avalanche rescue was based on the personal recital of an officer of the Tyrolean Gendarmerie who took part in a similar episode. The annual ski race is of particular interest in light of Bemelmans's own creation of such an event in Lech. In April 1948 Bemelmans told Massee in a letter that he had just instituted "a race for children, to be run after this annually, on Lincolns [*sic*] Birthday," for which he was providing prizes.[16] An enclosed clipping from the Austrian press noted that his purpose was "to help promote further talent among our youth, to spur them on to best effort" and that a local Olympic Ski Champion would be a judge.[17] In his letter Bemelmans spoke of his desire to see the d'Aulaires's *Abraham Lincoln* translated into German so that copies of the book might be distributed to all Austrian and German children: "I wished I could give them something to read that would do them a little good and teach them something about the U.S. . . . . I don't think hungry people can be thought [sic] democracy [*sic*] I am sure it has to be wanted rather than thought [*sic*], but I am sure that if anything would do good, a lovely book like the one about Lincoln given into a childs [*sic*] hand, would do as much as anything" (letter of April 1948).[18] The comment suggests Bemelmans's admiration for the book that had won the Caldecott in the year *Madeline* was runner-up. It also underscores his affection for children and his belief in the importance of their reading.

The High World is suited to adults and to older rather than younger children, as some critics noted at the time.[19] As with *Hansi* and *The Golden Basket,* the work might be described as an amply illustrated text rather than a picturebook. Unlike these earlier stories, however, *The High World* has no clear child protagonist: the story focuses on the conflict between Herr Oberministerialrat and the Amrainers, with Christopher serving as a catalyst to this action. Possibly today's child would find its descriptions of the Tyrol too didactic and slow-paced. Yet, the book contains a charm and a clarity of story line lacking in some of Bemelmans's other works for young readers. The writing is filled with sensory imagery and exhibits a sure sense of rhythm, as in this description of the Amrainer's meal time:

> Most of the time, their humble meal was a kind of porridge steaming in a large, black cast-iron pan. On Sundays a pat of butter was put in the center of it. The children who sat around the table with the parents, all eating out of the same pan, were busy with their spoons making depressions or tracing small channels in the mush, so as to lead some of the molten butter to their side. The advantage of this kind of cooking was that there weren't any dishes to wash and dry and put away. Everybody licked his spoon clean and stuck it into a wooden rack on the wall, and the pan in winter was cleaned with snow, and in summer with the sand of the brook that passed close to the house. (*HW,* 2–4)

Parsley

As the 1950s approached the midway mark, Bemelmans continued his prolific outpouring of works for adults and children. In 1955, the same year that he produced *Madeline's Christmas in Texas* for Neiman Marcus, he published his second juvenile with Harper & Brothers, *Parsley*. In 1980 the work was reprinted in English, and Afrikaans and Zulu editions appeared in Africa (Pomerance, 160). Its brief text and painterly illustrations stress themes of friendship and nature.

Bemelmans used the *Parsley* story twice before finally presenting it in picturebook form. He introduced its essential elements in one paragraph of *Father, Dear Father* (1953) as the "absolutely original" children's story of a Tyrolean inn-sitter named Wendelin. According to Wendelin, the story needed "a little polishing, and somebody to illustrate it" (*Father*, 58). Unless Bemelmans created the story himself and attributed it to Wendelin, he is thus indebted to this relatively anonymous fellow for the plot outline of one of his better-known works. Not long after, in *Woman's Day* for January 1954, Bemelmans presented in one page the essential outline of the book to come, along with one colored illustration, under the title "The Old Stag and the Tree."[20]

Wendelin places his story "Hereabouts, in the high crags of the Alps" (*Father*, 57). Early in its development, then, *Parsley* was Tyrolean, and the book thus represents the third and last time that Bemelmans turned to this region as inspiration for a juvenile work. In its final form, however, Bemelmans sets the story in North America, identifying the furniture created from the trees as "New England pine furniture" in a note at the back of the book.[21] Nevertheless, because most of the pictures are of mountains and forest, the setting seems universal.

The stag, an animal closely associated with the Tyrol, figures prominently in the story as it did in *Hansi* and *The High World*. In fact, the front of the hardcover presents the identical image of the stag used on a title page of *The High World*, Bemelmans's previous Harper publication. In the two earlier versions of *Parsley* Bemelmans leaves the stag unnamed: Wendelin calls the protagonist "a [or "the"] papa deer" (*Father*, 57, 58), and the *Woman's Day* version refers to him as "a [or "the"] stag" or "the old stag" (20). In the book itself, Bemelmans calls the stag Parsley or Old Parsley because of his well-known fondness for this herb, to which he attributes the animal's longevity.

At the outset of *Parsley* Bemelmans develops the original "Wendelin story" by elaborating on the importance of the "old/lone pine tree" (*P*, 6) as a principal character. While still a baby, standing at the edge of an abyss, the pine had recognized the hardships of nature; "And so it held onto the rocks / with a will" (*P*, 12). Because "it grew twisted and low to the ground" (*P*, 12), it outlasted several generations of other trees that were cut down and made into a variety of useful objects. In the shelter of its boughs, an old stag raised his family: "And the tree and the stag were / grateful to each other / and both grew very, very old" (*P,* 22). Into this harmony a hunter comes one day, intent on killing Parsley. As the hunter leans against the old pine to take aim, the wind blows, and the tree trips him. As the hunter is falling over the cliff, the pine thoughtfully procures the intruder's binoculars for Parsley, who now has only to look through them into the valley below to see danger before it arrives.

Bemelmans breaks *Parsley*'s short, unrhymed text into one short passage per page turn, further dividing these segments into lines of three to eight words. Opposite each such group of words, on the right-hand side of the double-page spread, there appears a full-page picture. The slow pace thus engendered contributes to a sense of peace. The illustration of so few words per page turn also permits much of the story to be told through the pictures; the final hunter sequence can be "read" without the text, almost as a series of stills on a piece of film.

The book owes its longevity in great measure to its large, painterly illustrations, all in full color, and offered for sale at the Hammer Galleries.[22] Done in gouache, these present a considerable variety of style and composition. From page to page, Bemelmans contrasts cool and warm colors, or a dramatically expressionistic treatment of nature with one that is delicately decorative. For instance, on the first page the old pine stands starkly glowing in the moonlight at the edge of the abyss, illustrating the words "At the edge of a deep, a deep / green forest stands an old / lone pine tree looking out / over the valley below" (*P,* 6). The composition consists of several strong, simple shapes—a diagonal wall of dark green pine, the night sky, a rectangular block of valley below, and the sheer wall of the cliff, all focusing attention on the gaunt shape of the tree's skeleton centered in the page and pointing to the oval moon. In contrast to these simple shapes and dark night colors, the lower two-thirds of the next page is filled with intriguing tiny details of a forest scene in the gray morning light to illustrate the pine's first tender days: "The tree had started life there / emerald green and hopeful / and for a while it stretched its / little arms unworried to the sky" (*P,* 8). Blue flowers, individually drawn, Bemelmans's typical standing rabbits, a horned owl, several deer, and one large snail are grouped around the tiny baby pine tree centered at the bottom; the scene's decorative quality is enhanced by a border of red ladybugs. Later in the book, another whimsical forest scene—the entire surface covered with individual images of birds, flowers, and gay animals—brings to mind a medieval tapestry.

In several images Bemelmans heightens the similarity of the pine boughs to the deer's antlers in order to suggest visually the harmony of the old pine and Parsley. In the cluster of forms on page 2, just described, boughs resemble deer antlers, teasing the eye to discern one from the other in a "hidden pictures" fashion. This illustration anticipates the later assurance: "And when the old tree and the / stag were together, / weatherbeaten the one and / gray the other, / it was difficult to tell / which were the antlers and / which were the barren boughs" (*P*, 28). The illustration for this text visually suggests their emotional bond: silhouetted against the glowing sunset, Parsley's antlers and the tree's gnarled branches seem to unite in one body. On the last page, Parsley's antlers and the pine's boughs alike house birds and other happy creatures.

Not long into the story, Bemelmans diverges from his central narrative to explain what happens to the other forest trees but does not happen to the crooked old pine. For eight pages he devotes text and pictures to aspects of the Northeastern lumber industry, depicting trees being felled in the forest, cut into boards at a sawmill, made into "furniture, / ships, toys, wagons, bridges, / matches, paper" (*P*, 18) at a carpenter's shop, and, finally, used as the walls of a house and "kindling, / and logs for the fireplace" (*P*, 20). This sequence is much expanded from the magazine version, thus suggesting Bemelmans's conscious adaptation of his story to a young audience. Although eight pages seems a bit long for what is essentially a narrative tangent, these pages do balance and anticipate the final hunter sequence, by presenting a human intrusion—albeit a much happier one—into the life of the forest.

The six pictures within the 12-page hunting sequence are bold in composition and color. The hunter himself is ugly and dehumanized, with binoculars instead of eyes, held by hands that look almost like hooks. The illustrations of the hunter pulling himself up the cliff, leaning against the tree to shoot Old Parsley, falling at the tree's base, and then tumbling over the cliff use a variety of bold perspectives to heighten the sense of danger. The cartooned image of the hunter's two boots disappearing off the bottom of the page accompanied by the words "Good-by—my luck she is running out!" (*P*, 40) suggest his impending death. The text evades this resolution by saying somewhat enigmatically, "he lay far below— / to hunt no more, / with his gun lost in a ravine" (*P*, 42).

On each double-page spread the white space surrounding the small amount of text is softened by a watercolor sketch of a wildflower, a dif-

ferent variety of flower on each page. Bemelmans identifies these flowers
in a list at the back of the book, thus teaching his young readers their
names and doubtless satisfying the curiosity of adults as well.

This story is far less ambivalent in its appeal than are some of the
other books Bemelmans published in the juvenile market in the years
following the appearance of *Madeline.* Unlike *Sunshine,* for instance,
where situations and characters are more fully comprehensible to the
adult than to the child, in *Parsley* the personification of nature and the
didactic elements—the list of flowers and especially the rather elementary facts about the lumbering industry—clearly target a juvenile reader.

Despite *Parsley*'s positive affirmation of friendship and the beauty of
its illustrations, however, in one way the book is not fully satisfying for
children. Indeed, perhaps as one critic objected, "the valuing of animal
above human life makes it questionable even from an adult point of
view."[23] Eliminating the hunter rather than reforming or permanently
discouraging him through some other means conveys a momentary cal-
lousness to the man's fate. Perhaps, as critic Shelton L. Root, Jr., suggests, the lack of imagination that Bemelmans spoke of in the Caldecott
acceptance speech reveals itself here in an ability to work out a different
ending (Root, 9). In any event, the final resolution treats the hunter as
an impersonal source of evil rather than as a human being; like the winter winds, he is one more obstacle to survival. The author/illustrator cannot so successfully move the human creature out of the realm of the realistic as he does the stag and the tree—that is, the reader is willing to
believe, for the duration of the story, in a supportive friendship between
a tree and a stag, but she cannot so readily accept that a hunter—someone engaged in this real setting in a real human activity—is some form
of evil monster who deserves to be obliterated. A young reader cannot
help but feel relieved that the hunter is gone, and the story urges her to
be grateful for—or at least to overlook—the probable death of a human
being.

Unlike most of Bemelmans's works for young readers, *Parsley* contains
little humor. An exception is the final illustration of Parsley, with hoary
beard and eyebrows, peering through the hunter's binoculars. A similar
picture of the old stag, but without the binoculars, appears on the front
jacket cover. Thus, before even opening the book, the reader is introduced to the movement of the narrative.

The sole illustration that appears in the *Woman's Day* version was
never used in the book. Both its rectangular shape and its thematic subject matter—Parsley staring over the cliff through binoculars, while

other deer graze nearby—suggest that Bemelmans may have originally intended it for endpapers, which the finished book does not have. Or perhaps he created it to lie across the two-column presentation of the magazine version.

Parsley's binoculars are yet another way of seeing, of affecting an image. They reveal Bemelmans's continuing fascination with ways of creating and changing an image—a fascination that he had shown early in his career in the monocle, lorgnette, spectacles, mirrors, and camera in *The Golden Basket.*

Welcome Home!

During the five years between *Parsley* (1955) and *Welcome Home!* (1960), Bemelmans was intensely busy with the *Madeline* series and works for the adult market. *Welcome Home!,* his third Harper publication, is based upon a poem by Beverley Bogert, a well-known horseman with whom Bemelmans was acquainted.[24] This brief verse creates a fantasy in which, each year, daddy fox outwits the hounds and returns to his loving family after the hunt. The work appeared first under the title "Randy" in *Mademoiselle* for December 1959.[25] Neither the magazine version nor the book identfies the fox as "Randy," yet the similarity between this word and "Reynard," along with the fact that there is no other protagonist, suggests that this is the fox's name. The magazine spread, described as "a preview of his book . . . which Harper's will publish soon" (42), consists of all of the text except that included in the book's first three pages, but only six of the illustrations.

The verse and illustrations of *Welcome Home!* embellish the stereotype of the clever fox by depicting the animal's attitude toward the hunt as a strenuous but enjoyable game of wits. He appears first on the front cover, looking rakish in a green cap. Next the reader meets his family as the two fox cubs ask their mother, "What's that yelping in the yard? / And why do those dogs / Bark so hard?"[26] The mother's attitude is one of pride in her husband's skill; she tells her children that the foxhounds they hear are not ordinary dogs: "They are the famous / Holiday Hounds / That chase the fox / With leaps and bounds." Having had his toes powdered "With aniseed/And peppermint / And maybe / Other kinds of scent," the fox stops next to a creek and rids himself of this tracking device, using a leaf to wipe his feet. On two occasions the text refers to the fox as "sly" or "very sly," and we are assured that "People say / The sly fox / Always—gets away." After the hunt the fox slips back home, where his family pampers him. A smirk on his lips, he rests in bed, feeling superior and reading *The Chronicle: A Sporting Journal.*

Inasmuch as the solitary fox outwits these hosts of human and animal foes, and not just once but year after year, *Welcome Home!* constitutes a mild spoof of fox hunting. Bemelmans's caricatures underscore this impression. As the mounts jump their first hedge, one horseman lands awkwardly on his bottom in a posture reminiscent of the Central Park rider in *The Happy Place.* The hunters look fairly dull as they engage in the unsportsmanlike activity of powdering the fox's toes. The panting dogs are frantic as they back into porcupines and poke into beehives in their futile quest.

And yet, despite this gentle mockery of hunting to the horn, Bemelmans's tone is not consistently ironic. The first several lines of text in the book, which Bemelmans added to the magazine version, celebrate the excitement and splendor of a foxhunt: "Now on this happy holiday morn / The Huntsman blowing on his horn / Says, 'Buckle your spurs / Upon your feet / And come and join / this Glorious Meet.'" The sincerity of this invitation is underscored on the next page, where the verse reads, "Then mothers, fathers, girls and boys / Join this best of outdoor joys." One child is buttoned into her collar while another is placed on a horse. Significantly, the mention of "girls and boys" specifically addresses the book's juvenile audience.

Yet if the book's first two pages leave the reader unprepared for the mild irony of the rest of the work, the exuberance of both text and pictures throughout lighten the satiric tone all the more: the fox hunt, despite the folly and exhaustion involved, looks like great fun. The rhyming text rollicks along, and scenes are filled with galloping riders and packs of yelping hounds. The red coats of the hunters, the red tongues of the dogs, and the many scenes painted in warm tones communicate the intensity of the event. Surely, the book suggests, any flaws in an event so exciting are simply part of the hilarity.

Welcome Home! makes a number of traditional appeals to young readers. These include colorful pictures, a rhymed text, anthropomorphic characters, and scenes of the fox-family life. As in many other children's works, the book permits "the little guy" to outsmart his more powerful foes. The cyclical plot structure of the poem also belongs to the juvenile tradition. Bemelmans's illustrations enhance the readers' sense that the hunters' journey comes full circle. At the outset, horses and riders race away from left to right; by sundown they return slowly from right to left. In fact, the conclusion is a kind of double homecoming, for after the hunters have returned to their stately mansion, Bemelmans devotes six more pages to the fox's safe arrival at his humble hut. Two large illustrations reveal that his family's warm welcome makes his shack a place of great comfort. His children wipe his face and pour water for his feet, while his wife administers a tonic and brings him a sandwich in bed.

The fact that Bemelmans changed the title from "Randy" to *Welcome Home!* suggests his conscious decision to emphasize the sense of security communicated by the book's final pages. The name of the fox, however—the story's wily protagonist—would have given the work a much clearer focus. Although the words "welcome home" subtly signal the conclusion, through much of the book they seem unrelated to the action. This is, first of all, because they would logically be spoken by the fox's family, rather than by the fox himself, and the former appears in only one illustration before the conclusion. Second, during the several pages where the fox wife's voice is narrating the action, she is expressing no anxiety for her husband's safe return but is, instead, bragging about his skill. Thus, rather than reflecting a goal important to the characters themselves, the title seems forced on the work from the outside.

At the same time that *Welcome Home!* somewhat perfunctorily conforms to traditions of juvenile literature, it also addresses adults in ways less accessible to the young reader. For instance, an adult more likely has the knowledge necessary to appreciate the irony of the interior scenes of the foxes' home. On the wall hangs a still life of a dead chicken and an egg, presumably the kind of picture this predator enjoys. The mantlepiece displays duck decoys, and one baby fox tenderly feeds a carrot to a toy stuffed rabbit.

Even less available to children is the knowledge to challenge Bemelmans's treatment of a blood sport as jolly fun for everyone. Admittedly, the text admits that for the fox this is a brush with death: "He knows he's running for his life, / He loves his children and his wife." For this reason, even the final line leaves one somewhat unsettled: "The Mother cries and says / 'My dear— / I think you're safe for / One more / Year.'" The fourleaf clovers and horseshoes on the front cover suggest the fox's need for luck. Foxes are often, if not always, killed in fox hunts; yet the book suggests otherwise: "The sly fox / Always—gets away." An adult with only a vague knowledge of the practices of fox hunting must suspect this cannot universally be so. A child may be misled.

The most satisfying aspect of *Welcome Home!* lies in its pictures, clearly the product of the intensified interest in studio painting that, according to *My Life in Art,* began in 1953. As was frequently the case with the art he created for his children's books, Bemelmans offered these works for sale in a Hammer Galleries exhibit (1–24 December 1960), which also included scenes of New York and the Mediterranean.[27] The book's 18 illustrations, including the cover, offer a visual variety that keeps the book unified yet lively. Some large rectangular illustrations are full color, while others have backgrounds of one color with black ink. Still others are sketches accented in red, brown, or gold. The light changes as the day progresses: the morning glows in gold, while the return home is bathed in red. The backgrounds of some of the outdoor scenes represent a new style in Bemelmans's children's books; beautiful, almost oriental-looking pheasants and other figures are outlined in thin black lines, or not at all, creating a soft contrast with the cartooned figures in the foreground. In yet another approach, the picture surface is covered with the intense horizontal streaks of a sunset, focusing attention on the fox, who, alone at last, returns home in the lower right-hand corner.

Although the artwork of *Welcome Home!* is exceptional, the illustrations alone cannot make up for a book that is ill-advised in its choice of a subject and consequently ambiguous in tone and focus. One surmises that the visual possibilities overly influenced the work's creation.

Marina

Bemelmans's last children's book, *Marina,* was published by Harper & Row in the year of his death, 1962. That same year, Viking published *On Board Noah's Ark*, an illustrated blend of fact and fiction that recounts a Mediterranean voyage on his newly purchased yacht. *Marina,* with its ocean setting and a name that suggests a yacht harbor, is a natural outgrowth of Bemelmans's intensified passion for the sea.

Marina is the name of the baby seal who is the protagonist of this short, rhymed work. Her father, "the Great O'Neil, the famous trained seal,"[28] leaves his job with the circus and moves his wife and daughter "to the sea and a shack that bore his name." While her father, a professional performer, complains about the "six purposeless porpoises" that he sees out in the ocean entertaining for free, Marina wanders into the water, and soons finds herself "in a / SHARK, / where it was awfully dark!" Her frantic father and mother ask the whale, the sea lion, and the alligator to help them rescue Marina, but each refuses. Then the six "clowns of the sea" go into action, lifting the shark "out of the ocean—a-one, a-two, a-three." Marina shoots out of the shark's mouth, and the porpoises continue to hold the villain out of the sea until he is nothing but an "old sharkskin." Marina's parents rush her off to the "Hospital of Physicians and Sturgeons," where she soon recovers.

The work has antecedents in Bemelmans's own cartoons about seals from nearly 30 years prior. "Noodles, the Trained Seal" made a one-time appearance in the *Saturday Evening Post* for April 1933.[29] "Silly Willy," also about a trained seal, appeared for two years on a weekly basis in *Young America* beginning in March 1935 (Pomerance, 267). Like *Marina* and much else that Bemelmans wrote for children, "Silly Willy" was in rhyme.

In a number of ways, *Marina* more specifically targets a juvenile audience than does any of the other post-*Madeline* books. Unlike most of these works, *Marina* did not appear in an adult magazine, and the book is the only one whose protagonist is clearly a child. In *Marina* Bemelmans returns to the plot formula that he had used in *Quito Express, Fifi,* and all the *Madeline* books: a vulnerable creature wanders into danger and has to be rescued by others more experienced. Following the literary norms of the time, Bemelmans never permits the threat to become overwhelming for his child reader. The fact that Marina wears her large yellow beach hat decorated with a red ribbon even in the belly of the shark comically reassures the reader that she has not lost her basic identity and that she will soon emerge. Like Madeline, Marina is rushed to the hospital. Perhaps surprisingly, unlike Madeline, Marina is shown in the operating room, surrounded by doctors and nurses standing next to a table full of knives and other surgical instruments. The frightening effect of such an image is mitigated, however, by the humorous sight of an octopus and four cranes in scrubs, and by a verse that assures us that the physician is the "famous Dr. Crane." After a page turn, the text and illustrations further comfort the child reader: "Miss Hippo Potamus, the registered nurse, / said, 'In my care nobody gets worse.'" On the very next page, "Marina was sitting up," and her parents bring her a bouquet of brightly colored sardines. Only five pages after entering the hospital, Marina returns home in her proud parents' loving care.

Other elements also suggest Bemelmans's primary focus on the child reader. The narrative structure involves repetition of an action: Marina's parents are turned down by three creatures in turn—the whale, the sea lion, and the alligator—before the porpoises come to their rescue. Furthermore, *Marina* offers an important message to a juvenile audience: the attendants who wave Marina good-bye at the hospital admonish her to "Remember, Marina, stay close to the shore! / And you won't have to come back here anymore!"

Unfortunately, however, the seriousness of this moral is somewhat masked by the fact that Bemelmans permits Marina's father, the Great O'Neil, to identify another point as the story's "great lesson": "When all the rest of the world lets you down, / your life may depend upon help from a clown." Fiddle, Faddle, Diddle, Daddle, Fuddle, and Duddle all rise from the sea, smiles on their friendly faces. The words, uttered by one who had at first scorned the porpoises, suggest his realization of their good qualities. The vague point they make, however, hardly constitutes a useful "lesson" for a child reader. Typically, the sun shines brightly on what was to be the last page of Bemelmans's last book for children.

Somewhat unexpected in a book for children is the picture of the porpoises holding the shark out of the water —even after he has released Marina—just in order to ensure his death. The sun beats down hotly, and the six porpoises, still smiling, lift the shark over their heads. The description of the death process is glibly detailed: "He shivered a while and he shrank and dribbled. / The old sharkskin was done for and shriveled."

Marina's watercolor cartoon illustrations lack the beauty of the pictures in Bemelmans's previous Harper books, *The High World, Parsley,* and *Welcome Home!* Bemelmans adds interest with bright colors—red, yellow, blue, and green—and touches of visual humor. For instance, Mr. O'Neil wears a flashy beach shirt, while his wife wears a hula skirt. The endpapers show Marina below the sea sweetly exploring the world of exotic fish and other forms of underwater life, as the shark floats menacingly by above her, thus signaling her dangerous adventure.

Marina's bouncing verse and bright colors, the jolly porpoises, the circus and ocean settings, and an appealing baby protagonist add up to a pleasing, if relatively inconsequential book.

Chapter Five

Madeline: Modern More than Fifty Years Later

Madeline in New Formats

In the 1990s interest remains very high in the *Madeline* books. Following Bemelmans's own example of energetic marketing, Viking produced four new *Madeline* books in the 1980s and 1990s. Beginning with the "discovery" of *Madeline's Christmas* in 1985, the publisher next presented a *Madeline Pop-Up* (1987) based on the original *Madeline,*[1] and *Madeline's House* (1989), a box in the shape of a house containing miniatures of the first three books in the series.[2] In 1993, there appeared *Mad about Madeline,* a large-format edition of all six works (the original series plus *Madeline's Christmas*).[3] In addition to these new books, Madeline lovers can also purchase an ever-increasing variety of dolls, toys, and puzzles, as well as audio- and videocassettes.

Over the years, *Madeline* has been translated into many languages. A 1985 small-format French paperback entitled *Madeleine* not only rhymes, but it has somehow corrected one of Bemelmans's mistakes. In the original *Madeline,* in the last picture of the little girls "breaking bread" at the dinner table, Bemelmans drew 12 children where there should only have been 11, Madeline herself being away in the hospital. In the French version, a twelfth girl has been removed; however, apparently because of difficulties of erasure, the one removed was not the one standing in Madeline's usual place.[4]

As noted in Chapter 3, for many years, little girls have been dressed by their parents "à la Madeline," particularly with respect to her distinctive yellow hat. As recently as 1988, the Smithsonian Institution advertised wearable replicas for sale.[5]

Color television—the medium Bemelmans celebrated in 1947 in *A Tale of Two Glimps*—has proved to be one of his biggest allies in bringing his stories to a mass audience. Currently, animated versions are broadcast frequently, and video cassette recordings are available for home consumption.

Becoming a Classic

A "classic" can be described as a work that is read and known by a great many people over many years. By this definition, the works in the *Madeline* series, and particularly the original *Madeline* (1939), are clearly "classics." After *Madeline's Rescue* (1953), Bemelmans, through the multiple marketing techniques described in Chapter 3, proceeded to make Madeline a household name. Having gained critical as well as popular approval with the first two books, he kept his heroine before the public in magazines, art galleries, various media presentations, and, most important, new books in the Viking series. By now, more than 50 years later, four generations are enjoying *Madeline* in one form or another. In 1985, at the time of the publication of *Madeline's Christmas, Publishers Weekly* noted that the books in the *Madeline* series had "a combined in-print total of more than five million copies in the United States alone and have been translated into many languages."[6]

The *Madeline* books continue to be popular because, in many senses, they are very contemporary. Perhaps the appeal of *Madeline* in 1939 to readers of all ages and the growing popularity of the series through the years influenced picturebook norms in such a way that the books helped create their own future acceptance. Elements that Bemelmans was among the first to introduce and that continue to be popular today include cartooning and a playfulness about "story" and reality. *Madeline* also broke ground with its humorous nonmoralizing mood and its use of color. In addition to these far-reaching innovations, the books present situations, characters, and settings that happen to correspond very neatly to trends in picturebook publishing which have emerged in response to social changes over the years since *Madeline's* first appearance. The erosion of the family and the improved status of women and minorities have resulted in many children's books with one or more parents absent, with female protagonists or with foreign settings. Finally, in rhyming his text, Bemelmans intuitively followed a centuries-old practice of literature for young children whose popularity has not dimmed in present-day publishing. For all of these reasons *Madeline* is perfectly at home in the 1990s.

Critic Zohar Shavit's discussion of the ability of "ambivalent texts" to become classics by shaping picturebook norms as "models of imitation"[7] has some relevance to this analysis of *Madeline's* ability to effect change. In *The Poetics of Children's Literature,* Shavit uses the term "ambivalent texts" to mean "texts [that] belong simultaneously to more than one [literary] system and consequently are read differently (though concurrently), by at least two groups of readers. Those groups of readers diverge in their expectations, as well as in their norms and habits of reading. Hence their realization of the same text will be greatly different" (66). Elsewhere Shavit notes that an ambivalent text may appeal "primarily to adults, using the child as an excuse rather than as a real addressee" (63). In her discussion she concentrates primarily on children's texts that have to be abridged or rewritten in order to make them completely comprehensible to children, using *Alice in Wonderland* as a test case (71–91). This is not the case with *Madeline;* as shown in Chapter 3, the child is at least equally *Madeline*'s addressee, and not an "excuse." Nevertheless, in *Madeline* Bemelmans did in some ways make a clear appeal to contemporary adult tastes, and in the process violated existing esthetic standards for children's picturebooks. Because *Madeline* was and continues to be such a runaway success with both adults and children, it is reasonable to argue that the book exerted an influence for change, providing a "model of imitation" of certain of its unorthodox features.

As noted, one of Bemelmans's most dramatic departures from contemporary juvenile norms was the use of cartooning, a popular feature of sophisticated adult magazines at the time. Most of the illustrations for children's picturebooks up until Bemelmans's time were realistic; in fact, according to Barbara Bader, the comic strips were regarded with horror by children's librarians, and not only because such terrors as the Katzenjammer Kids provided improper models of behavior, but also because the artwork was regarded as substandard, not the esthetic fare upon which children should be nourished (Bader, 2–12).[8] For instance, Bader points out that W. W. Denslow, the original illustrator of *The Wizard of Oz,* received scathing comment from Anne Carroll Moore in 1905 for his nonrepresentational drawing: "Such books as Denslow's *Mother Goose* . . . with a score of others of the comic poster order, should be banished from the sight of impressionable small children."[9] Certainly, this seems to have been May Massee's view, as reflected in Bemelmans's early struggles to overcome "cartoonitis" in the early stages of *Hansi.*

Although *Madeline* was not the first enduring picturebook with cartoon illustrations, it was among them. In the 1930s, in France, Jean de Brunhoff began turning out stories of Babar the Elephant in rapid succession, using a distinctive cartooning style, and occasionally inserting an additional verbal message through the comic strip device of the speech balloon, a technique employed also by England's Edward Ardizzone in the Little Tim series. In 1937, in America, advertising cartoonist Theodor Seuss Geisel ("Quick, Henry, the Flit!")[10] published *And to Think That I Saw It on Mulberry Street,* thus beginning a long career of entertaining young readers with the antics of normal children and wildly imaginative creatures. In the 1940s Austrian immigrant H. A. Rey presented one of America's most famous animal children, Curious George, a lovable trouble-finder who also appeared in *Good Housekeeping* magazine under the name "Zozo."[11] Somewhat later, in 1959, Bernie Wiseman, who remembers working at the *New Yorker* at some point when Bemelmans was there, began entertaining young readers with the adventures of Morris the Moose.[12] Significantly, the works of all of these author/illustrators have remained in print for several decades, a remarkable achievement in today's publishing world.

Thus not on its own merits alone, but in conjunction with these other works, *Madeline* has been influential in urging the acceptance of a cartooning style in children's books. At the same time that the public has embraced a less representational style, so, too, has critical acceptance increased. Dr. Seuss has been Caldecott runner-up three times: in 1948 for *McElligot's Pool,* in 1950 for *Bartholomew and the Oobleck,* and in 1951 for *If I Ran the Zoo.* His *The 500 Hats of Bartholomew Cubbins* (1938) is included on the Touchstones List of the Children's Literature Association. Maurice Sendak, one of America's most applauded contemporary creator of children's picturebooks, himself employed a cartooning style and even a modified comic-strip panel approach in his 1971 Caldecott Honor Book, *In the Night Kitchen,* a work whose protagonist he named after one of his childhood heroes, Walt Disney's Mickey Mouse.[13] William Steig is an even more recent example of an author/cartoonist who has earned Caldecott approval for his books: the 1970 Medal for *Sylvester and the Magic Pebble,* and the 1977 Honor Award for *The Amazing Bone.*

Despite the increased acceptance of cartooning as "good" children's book art, however, the representational esthetic still holds the upper hand. The vast majority of Caldecott winners achieve a greater realism than the above mentioned artists. This is due, in part, to the didactic goal of teaching young readers what the world looks like. Perhaps, too, critics and parents fail to appreciate the skill that goes into capturing the essence of a personality or a movement in a line or two.

A second aspect of *Madeline* in which Bemelmans initially depended on the acceptance of his adult reader was its playful treatment of reality and illusion. For instance, the framing effects that Bemelmans used in

Madeline's endpapers essentially force upon the reader a consciousness of the book as art. In presenting *Madeline* as illusion, Bemelmans broke with the existing juvenile norm; for according to Patricia Dooley, in keeping with the Western "window in the wall" tradition of the framed easel painting, frames have traditionally been used in children's books to enhance the reader's belief in the reality of the experience.[14] Peggy Whalen Levitt points to a number of works—from Crockett Johnson's *Harold and the Purple Crayon* (1955) to Monique Félix's *The Story of a Little Mouse Trapped in a Book* (1980)—that "break frame" in ways that play with reality and illusion; she includes in her discussion the work of Tomi de Ungerer, Lester Abrams, Richard Egielski, and John S. Goodall.[15] Bemelmans's nonrepresentational and highly patterned illustrations, formulaic verse, and such devices as playing with type size to suggest the trailing off of the narrator's voice all emphasize the distance between *Madeline* and the reader's own reality. The popularity of the *Madeline* books ultimately helped pave the way for acceptance of approaches to the separate world of story as sophisticated as that of David Macaulay's 1991 Caldecott Medal winner, *Black and White*.

In its refusal to impart a moral, *Madeline* is a kind of *Alice in Wonderland* of the history of the picturebook. Linda Kauffman Peterson and Marilyn Leathers Solt, in *Newbery and Caldecott Medal and Honor Books,* observe that *Madeline* is "one of the first early Award Books to introduce a digression from the sedate, low-keyed books that dominate the early years of the Caldecott Medal."[16] In the 1930s and 1940s "edification" was a dominant picturebook motivation. Such winners as Fish/Lathrop's *Animals of the Bible* (1937), Handforth's *Mei Li* (1938), the d'Aulaires's *Abraham Lincoln* (1939), and Lawson's *They Were Strong and Good* (1940) impart not only factual information but also moral values. In *Madeline,* however, although the illustrations communicate information about Paris, the story itself insists very little upon any lesson it might incidentally convey. When *Madeline* first appeared, May Lamberton Becker commented, "I suppose there's a moral; I didn't look for it. I was too busy laughing. This is fun that won't go out of style."[17] Her comment is both revealing and prophetic. The humorous, sometimes anthropomorphic treatment of real situations by authors such as Arnold Lobel, Audrey and Don Woods, Stephen Kellogg, and Rosemary Wells suggests that a nondidactic approach to life's difficulties is popular with today's readers. The late James Marshall—illustrator of the George and Martha books, *Miss Nelson Is Missing,* and other funny works—found in Bemelmans a kindred spirit: "I love Ludwig

Bemelmans' *Madeline* books. He also worked in a sort of frenzied, almost sloppy way and his illustrations are very energetic."[18]

One of the most obvious ways in which Bemelmans differed from the early Caldecott winners was his striking use of color. If color was used sparingly in the 1930s, it was not primarily for esthetic reasons but for reasons of economics and technology. Dorothy Lathrop, illustrator of Helen Dean Fish's *Animals of the Bible* (1937); Thomas Handforth in *Mei Li* (1938); Robert Lawson in *They Were Strong and Good* (1940); and Robert McCloskey in *Make Way for Ducklings* (1941) use either black or brown and white. Bemelmans, like Ingri and Edgar Parin d'Aulaire in *Abraham Lincoln* (1939), used full color on only a limited number of pages of *Madeline,* opting for an energizing yellow for the majority of the illustrations. The success of the *Madeline* series as well as of books by the d'Aulaires, Virginia Lee Burton, Maud and Miska Petersham, and Clement Hurd no doubt accelerated publishers' eagerness to find the means of easier, less expensive, and more faithful color reproduction in use today. Without question, Bemelmans's use of color has contributed to the *Madeline* books' durability, for color is the norm in the 1990s, rather than the exception. Decades later he continues to inspire comparison, as in a 1986 review of Amy Schwartz's illustrations for *The Purple Coat:* "The glowing watercolors are reminiscent of Bemelmans."[19]

One of the most striking ways in which *Madeline* pioneered contemporary picturebook norms was in having a female protagonist. Other innovative works in this regard were Thomas Handforth's *Mei Li* (1938), which won the Caldecott the year Madeline was published, and Gertrude Stein's *The World Is Round* (1939), a work that, Madeleine Bemelmans notes, "amused" her husband.[20] Although none has achieved the recognition of Madeline, girl protagonists have appeared regularly in the last 50 years in Caldecott Medal and Honor Award winners, beginning with Sal of McCloskey's *Blueberries for Sal* (1948) and *One Morning in Maine* (1952). In the 1960s Maurice Sendak illustrated Charlotte Zolotow's unnamed giftgiver in *Mr. Rabbit and the Lovely Present* (1962), and Eveline Ness created the introspective heroine of *Sam, Bangs & Moonshine* (1966). After Paul Goble's *The Girl Who Loved Wild Horses* (1978), the number of female protagonists in Caldecott winners increased rapidly during the 1980s. Maurice Sendak depicted a female rescuer in Ida of *Outside over There* (1981). Author Cynthia Rylant remembered her childhood in two books: *When I Was Young in the Mountains* (1982; illustrated by Diane Goode) and *The Relatives Came* (1985; illustrated by Stephen Gammell). Several books depicting female minority members also won awards: Vera B. Williams's *A Chair for My Mother* (1982); Patricia McKissack's *Mirandy and Brother Wind* (1988, illustrated by Jerry Pinkney); and Faith Ringgold's *Tar Beach* (1991).

In 1955 Kay Thompson and Hilary Knight presented *Eloise: A Work for Precocious Grown Ups.* Although the book invites comparison to *Madeline,* as its subtitle suggests, it more clearly appeals to an adult reader, who may be fascinated by the many ingenious things an inventive child can do to annoy adults in a hotel.

Read-aloud advocate Jim Trelease, who notes that the *Madeline* books are "among the favorites of children around the world," recommends a "related book" with another saucy female protagonist, Mercer Mayer's *Liza Lou and the Yeller Belly Swamp* (1976).[21]

Certainly *Madeline* cannot claim most of the credit for the increased presence of female protagonists in picturebooks; the women's movement has greatly influenced all the norms of children's book publishing, altering the extent to which girls and women are depicted, as well as their activities, personalities, and roles. Without question, however, the fact that *Madeline* has a female protagonist is one reason for the book's contemporary appeal. More than 50 years later, Emily Arnold McCully's heroine of the 1993 Caldecott Medal winner *Mirette on the High Wire* has Madeline's own penchant for doing the unconventional in Paris. She even has the same red hair.

Curiously, Madeline's appeal in this era of changing attitudes toward women is ambivalent—that is, readers can find in her whichever interpretation of the ideal female personality they prefer. To some she is the independent, brave, assertive female; Bernice Cullinan, for instance, calls her "one of the earliest derring-do females."[22] This is true, of course, particularly in *Madeline and the Bad Hat,* where Madeline rescues the cat and later saves Pepito from his dangerous excesses. It is true, too, in the non-canonical *Madeline's Christmas,* in which Madeline cares for her sick friends and governess, even taking the initiative to buy the Magician's magic carpets. And it is even true in the original *Madeline,* where "To the tiger in the zoo / Madeline just said, 'Pooh-pooh.'" On the other hand, Madeline is so small—"the smallest one was Madeline"—and so naive about what dangers lurk out there, that for the reader who prefers to see in her a "helpless female," complete with neat white gloves and hat, she can present this image, too. Her need to be rescued is a principal conflict in most of the books. The adult reader, in particular, need only identify with Miss Clavel to take Madeline less than seriously as an independent being.

Simply by depicting the existence he and his mother had known as European boarding school children, Bemelmans introduced an element of emotional isolation that is far more prevalent in today's picturebooks than it was earlier in the century. Although it is a fairly standard device for a child hero to leave his family as he experiences danger, in the 1930s and 1940s biological relatives were generally present at some point. The family or family members so prominent in such books as Flack/Wiese's *The Story about Ping* (1933), Leaf/Lawson's *The Story of Ferdinand* (1936), and McCloskey's *Blueberries for Sal* (1948) have been replaced in *Madeline,* however, by companions and a surrogate parent. In the 1960s and 1970s Ezra Jack Keats's picturebooks are of special note among those emphasizing the child's existence apart from his family. Today, in an age of latchkey children and divorce, the absence of parents in *Madeline* is a situation reflected in many works for elementary-school-age and younger readers.

Another category of today's picturebooks into which *Madeline* fits comfortably is that of realistic problem fiction. Current books for youngsters explore every kind of potentially upsetting situation from fear of a new babysitter to coping with divorce or death. It is Madeline's trip to the hospital in the first book and her loss of a beloved pet in the second—crises that occur in many young lives—that make these two books the most gripping of the series. The threatening situations in the last three—having to defend a cat, being kidnapped by gypsies, and being carried away by a runaway horse—are either less compelling or less likely than the first two. Nevertheless, each book in the original series permits a young reader to confront danger or separation in an organized, beautiful, and clearly fictional world. Perhaps it is no coincidence that Judy Blume, widely selling author of realistic fiction for juvenile readers, professes a special love for *Madeline* when she was younger. Thinking the library copy was the only copy in the world, she hid it, for "There was no way I was going to part with *Madeline.*"[23]

As discussed in Chapter 3, *Madeline* was published in an era when realistic picturebooks with foreign settings were popular. Although the attention paid to this type of book has vacillated over the last half-century (Peterson and Solt, 230), as children's book publishing enters the last decade, multiculturalism is an increasingly important trend. A steady rise in global awareness and attention to minorities within the United States has made books about other cultures popular and profitable. Thus, in the *Madeline* books, the depiction of the physical locale and customs of France, Paris, and London enhances their marketability. The basically unchanged settings, as well as the timeless clothing of nuns, *gendarmes,* and London bobbies, all contribute to the books' contemporary appeal.

Without doubt, one of the most essential ingredients of *Madeline*'s continuing popularity is its rhymed text. In this regard, Bemelmans was not a catalyst for change; rather, he simply recognized children's delight in rhyme and rhythm as authors and illustrators had done for centuries before him. From its inception to the present, the Caldecott has honored illustrators of songs and poems, including Maud and Miska Petersham, Marguerite de Angeli, Feodor Rojankovsky, Peter Spier, Evaline Ness, Susan Jeffers, and Alice and Martin Provensen. Bemelmans was, nevertheless, one of the first Caldecott honorees to employ rhyme throughout an original narrative, a practice that may have been inspired by his fondness for German author/artist Wilhelm Busch. A decade after *Madeline,* Theodor Geisel, who rhymed his way through many zany stories, won with *McElligot's Pool* (1947) and *If I Ran the Zoo* (1950). The 1965 Caldecott Medal winner, *May I Bring a Friend?,* written by Beatrice Schenk de Regniers and illustrated by Beni Montresor, and a 1970 Caldecott Honor Award winner, *The Judge: An Untrue Tale*, written by Harve Zemach and illustrated by Margot Zemach, have likewise used this engaging narrative style.

Verse continues to be popular in children's books at the close of the twentieth century. In fact, in the teaching of reading, there is emerging a whole new genre, "the predictable book," so named because it repeats one language pattern throughout, often in rhyme. Bernice Cullinan points to Bill Martin, Jr.'s rhyming *Brown Bear, Brown Bear, What Do You See?* ("I see a redbird looking at me") as "perhaps the one that accounts for the recognition of the type" (Cullinan, 119). While *Madeline* is not a predictable book in this narrowest sense, children have used it for years to practice the early reading skills by looking at the pictures and the words while saying aloud the rhymed and frequently repeated text.

Both because the *Madeline* books were on the cutting edge of change in many picturebook norms, and because they retain what children have delighted in for centuries, they are remarkably at home in the last decade of the twentieth century. The works appear in the bookstores in an environment where they have much in common with more recently created wares in terms of their artistry, purpose, and protagonist. The gaiety, energy, and beauty of all the books, as well as the creative activities of their promoters, will keep them in readers' hands for years to come.

Notes and References

Preface

1. Madeleine Bemelmans, letter to author, 13 July 1988.
2. "Madeline's Master," *Newsweek,* 15 October 1962, 115; hereafter cited in text.
3. Robert Van Gelder, "An Interview with Ludwig Bemelmans," *New York Times Book Review,* 26 January 1941, 2; hereafter cited in text.
4. Madeleine Bemelmans, letter to author, 12 June 1991.

Chapter One

1. May Massee, "Caldecott Award to Bemelmans," *Library Journal* 79 (15 March 1954): 485; hereafter cited in text.
2. Robert L. Berner, "Bemelmans, Ludwig," *Dictionary of American Biography,* (supp. 7, 1961–65), ed. John A. Garraty (New York: Scribners, 1981), 48; hereafter cited in text.
3. I am using the date given by Madeleine Bemelmans in her Introduction to *Tell Them It Was Wonderful: Selected Writings by Ludwig Bemelmans,* ed. Madeleine Bemelmans, foreword by Norman Cousins (New York: Viking Press, 1985), xvi; hereafter cited in text. Various dates have been given.
4. "Swan Country," in *My Life in Art* (New York: Harper & Brothers, 1958), 7–24; hereafter cited in text.
5. "Lausbub," in *Tell Them,* 26–27; hereafter cited in text.
6. Henry C. Pitz, "Ludwig Bemelmans," *American Artist* 15 (May 1951): 49; hereafter cited in text.
7. Madeleine Bemelmans, letter to author, 5 September 1994.
8. "Arrival in America," in *Tell Them,* 28.
9. "The Old Ritz," in *Tell Them,* 158; hereafter cited in text. Bemelmans also wrote humorously of his early efforts to be a cartoonist in "Art at the Hotel Splendide." *New Yorker,* 1 June 1940, 28–32.
10. "Illustrator: Man about Town Tries His Hand at Many Trades," *Newsweek,* 24 July 1937, 21; hereafter cited in text.
11. "Thrilling Adventures of Count Bric a Brac," *Milwaukee Journal,* 19 and 26 September; 3, 10, 17, 24, and 31 October; 7, 14, 21, and 28 November; 5 and 12 December (all Sundays in 1926); hereafter cited in text.
12. Bill Blackbeard, telephone interview, 6 August 1991; hereafter cited in text.
13. This story is told a number of places. One of the most informative versions is Massee, 484. Bemelmans describes their meeting in "The Old Ritz"

(161) and also in "May Massee as Her Author-Illustrators See Her," *Hornbook* 12 (July–August 1936): 231; hereafter cited in text.

14.   Madeleine Bemelmans notes that Barbara was born the year after the trip to Bruges, which occurred in 1935 (*Tell Them*, xvii).

15.   Murray Pomerance, *Ludwig Bemelmans: A Bibliography* (New York: Heineman, 1993), 267; hereafter cited in text.

16.   *Time,* 21 November 1938, 70.

17.   "A Trip to Bruges," *Vogue,* September 1936, 88–89; hereafter cited in text.

18.   Lee Rogow, "A Younger Bemelmaniac," *Saturday Review,* 29 August 1953, 13.

19.   "Stars Breaking Through," *Vogue,* 15 August 1939, 106.

20.   A sketch he drew of himself in uniform is included in a letter he wrote to New York children's librarian Anne Carroll Moore. The letter is with her papers at the New York Public Library, Mid-Manhattan branch.

21.   "Dear General—What a Surprise!" *Town and Country,* August 1939, 61. This article appeared soon after in *Small Beer*.

22.   Jay Martin, *Nathanael West: The Art of His Life* (New York: Farrar, Straus & Giroux, 1970), 298–301. See also Dennis P. Vannatta, *Nathanael West: An Annotated Bibliography of the Scholarship and Works* (New York: Garland, 1976). Vannatta notes that the play was never published (157).

23.   Hume Cronyn, *A Terrible Liar: A Memoir* (New York: William Morrow, 1991), 213–18.

24.   "A Reviewer's Notebook" (*New York Times,* 12 November 1939, 9) notes that Bemelmans is exhibiting originals of his illustrations in pastel and in watercolor at Kennedy's.

25.   Nearly the complete text of "Swan Country" appeared two months earlier as "When You Lunch with the Emperor," in *Vogue,* 1 September 1958, 208–9+.

26.   "Bemelmans," Hammer Galleries exhibition brochure, 30 November through 31 December; probably in 1955, when *Parsley* appeared.

27.   "Bemelmans Paints New York," *Holiday,* October 1959, 64–71.

28.   This dummy of *Hansi* is located in the files of the children's area of the Donnell branch of the New York Public Library.

29.   "Bemelmans," *Current Biography: Who's News and Why, 1941,* ed. Maxine Block (New York: H. W. Wilson, 1941), 62.

30.   May Massee, "Ludwig Bemelmans Biographical Paper," *Caldecott Medal Books: 1938–1957, with the Artist's Acceptance Papers and Related Material Chiefly from the "Horn Book Magazine,"* Horn Book Papers, vol. 2, ed. Bertha Mahony Miller and Elinor Whitney Field (Boston: Horn Book, 1957), 262.

31.   "People Watcher," *Time,* 31 March 1952, 74; hereafter cited in text.

32.   Norman Cousins, Foreword to *Tell Them*, vii.

33.   *Father, Dear Father* (New York: Viking, 1953), 92; hereafter cited in text.

34. *La Bonne Table,* sel. and ed. Donald and Eleanor Friede (New York: Simon & Schuster, 1964; Boston: David R. Godine, 1989), 17. Donald Friede was Bemelmans's editor for his last two novels—*Are You Hungry Are You Cold?* and *The Street Where the Heart Lies*—at World Publishing, where Eleanor worked in advertising.

35. "Home Splendide," *House and Garden,* August 1942, 21; hereafter cited in text. See also "Ludwig Bemelmans' Splendide Apartment," *Vogue,* 1 April 1942, 60–61; hereafter cited in text.

36. "Bemelmans," in *National Cyclopaedia of American Biography,* vol. 48 (Ann Arbor, Mich.: University Microfilms, 1967), 185.

37. "Ludwig Bemelmans Dies at 64; Writer-Artist Created Madeline," *New York Times,* 2 October 1962, 39.

38. *Madeline* (New York: Simon & Schuster, 1939; New York: New Viking Edition, 1960) unpaged; all quotations are from this edition.

39. "Monsieur Carnewal and the Start of the Story" [1936?], in *Writing Books for Boys and Girls: A "Young Wings" Anthology of Essays by Two Hundred Sixteen Authors Who Tell How They Came To Write Their Special Kinds of Books for Young Readers,* ed. Helen Ferris (Garden City, N.Y.: Junior Literary Guild; Doubleday, 1952), 85–87; hereafter cited in text.

40. "Art Class," in *Tell Them,* 66. Originally part of "Life Class" in *Life Class* (1938).

41. Ethel Heins, "Ludwig Bemelmans," in *Writers for Children: Critical Studies of Major Authors since the Seventeenth Century,* ed. Jane M. Bingham (New York: Scribners, 1988), 55, 58.

42. "And So Madeline Was Born" (Caldecott Award acceptance paper, 1954), *Caldecott Medal Books,* 255; hereafter cited in text.

43. "Art for Art's Sake," *Town and Country,* July 1945, 55; hereafter cited in text.

44. "Last Visit to Regensburg," in *Tell Them,* 312.

45. Letter of 29 October 1960 to Marcel Salinas, his assistant for *Madeline in London.*

46. Letter to Massee, 1 November 1949.

47. "Sunshine Sunshine Go Away: A Story about the City of New York," *Good Housekeeping,* December 1949, 76.

48. "Christmas in Tyrol," *Holiday,* December 1950, 170; hereafter cited in text.

49. Madeleine Bemelmans, letter to author, 31 July 1988.

50. Will Eisner, "Comics as a Form of Reading" and "Imagery," in *Comics and Sequential Art* (Tamarac, Fla.: Poorhouse Press, 1985), 7–24.

51. *The World Encyclopedia of Comics,* ed. Maurice Horn (New York: Chelsea House; London: New English Library, 1976), 486; hereafter cited in text. Horn cites Dieter Fuchs.

52. Wilhelm Busch, "Max and Moritz" (1865), trans. Walter Arndt, in *Wilhelm Busch and Others: German Satirical Writings,* ed. Dieter P. Lotze and Volkmar Sander (New York: Continuum, 1984), 41–42.

53. For a fuller discussion of Busch's satiric techniques, see Dieter P. Lotze's Introduction to *Wilhelm Busch and Others,* xv–xxvi.

Chapter Two

1. "Noodles, the Trained Seal," *Saturday Evening Post,* 29 April 1933, 22; "The Count and the Cobbler," *Harper's Bazaar,* December 1935, 52–53 (hereafter cited in text); "Transgressor in Galapagos," *Town and Country,* January 1939, 24–25; "True Love Story," *Town and Country,* October 1939.

2. New York Public Library, Donnell branch. This preliminary dummy was included in a copy of *Hansi* that Bemelmans signed for Anne Carroll Moore, the library's well-known supervisor of children's services, at Christmas, 1934.

3. No. 64, May Massee Collection, Emporia State University. This 24-page, full-color miniature outline dummy is glued inside the back lining of the copy of *Hansi* that Bemelmans presented to Massee. I am indebted to Curator Mary Bogan for describing this to me over the phone.

4. Letter to Massee, undated.

5. *Hansi* (New York: Viking, 1934), unpaged; all quotations are from this edition.

6. In Gary D. Schmidt, *Robert McCloskey* (Boston: Twayne, 1990), 8; cited in Ethel Heins, "From Mallards to Maine: A Conversation with Robert McCloskey," *Journal of Youth Services in Libraries* 1 (Winter 1988): 187–93.

7. No. 64, May Massee Collection, Emporia State University.

8. *Reading and the School Library* (May–June 1937): 177.

9. See Barbara Bader, *American Picturebooks from Noah's Ark to the Beast Within* (New York: Macmillan, 1976), especially chapters on "Wanda Gág" and "Foreign Backgrounds" (32–59); hereafter cited in text.

10. Massee informed Bemelmans of this necessity in a letter of 21 November 1945.

11. Anne T. Eaton, review of *Hansi, New York Times,* 11 November 1934, 24.

12. Letter to May Massee, 12 April 1935; hereafter cited in text.

13. Letter to May Massee, 8 May 1935.

14. "Book Marks" (probably from the *New York Herald Tribune,* sometime in September 1936); this clipping was found in the Bemelmans file in the New York Public Library, Donnell branch.

15. Linda Kauffman Peterson and Marilyn Leathers Solt, *Newbery and Caldecott Medal and Honor Books: An Annotated Bibliography* (Boston: G. K. Hall, 1982), 63; hereafter cited in text.

16. *The Golden Basket* (New York: Viking, 1936), 43; hereafter cited in text as *GB.*

17. *Madeline* (New York: Simon & Schuster, 1939; New York: New Viking Edition, 1960), unpaged; all quotations are from this edition.

18. An undated Viking release describes the anticipated trip of Bemelmans and his wife and says that "The little inn '*Au Panier d'Or*' in Bruges has been chosen as the setting for Mr. Ludwig Bemelmans' new children's book."

19. See Madeleine Bemelmans's Introduction to *Tell Them,* xix.

20. *The Castle Number Nine* (New York: Viking, 1937), unpaged; all quotations are from this edition.

21. Joseph Jacobs, "Master of All Masters," in *English Fairy Tales* (New York: Grosset & Dunlap, n.d.), 256–57.

22. Letter to Massee, from the *Santa Clara*, near Cristobal, undated (May 1937?). The book he refers to is Emil Ludwig's *The Nile: The Life-Story of a River,* trans. Mary H. Lindsay (New York: Viking, 1937).

23. Pomerance (186–87) notes that *Een Kerst Geschiedenis* is a Dutch version of "The Count and the Cobbler."

24. "Book Marks," clipping in the Bemelmans file, New York Public Library.

25. Letter to Massee, undated.

26. Letter to Massee, 21 May 1937, from Quito. The American Library Association had been seriously considering the establishment of a medal for picturebook artists since May 1936; the Caldecott was officially named and its terms described in a resolution on 24 June 1937. See Irene Smith, *A History of the Newbery and Caldecott Medals* (New York: Viking, 1957), 63–65.

27. Letter to Massee, 25 May 1937, from Ecuador.

28. Letter to Milton Glick, postmarked 7 July 1937, No. 62, May Massee Collection, Emporia State University. Although this letter is cataloged as part of the materials on *Castle Number Nine,* the date as well as interior evidence suggests that the book Bemelmans refers to is actually *My War with the United States. Castle* was not published until 1 November 1937, while *My War* appeared on 2 July (Pomerance, 45, 148). Decorating the letter with a celebratory cannon shooting out six cannonballs, Bemelmans praises the "good layout in title page!" and regrets that he is "sorry that I have only the six cannonballs to salute you with—you deserve the full 21." The title page of *My War,* as well as the front cover, shows a cannon similar to that on the letter, with a pile of six balls ready to be shot.

29. Letter to Massee, 1 November 1949.

30. Letter to Massee, 25 December 1937; hereafter cited in text.

31. Munro Leaf, *Noodle,* illus. Bemelmans (New York: F. A. Stokes, 1937), unpaged; all quotations are from this edition. Inside the front cover of a copy in the Anne Carroll Moore Collection at the New York Public Library, Donnell branch, are photographs of a dachshund, seemingly the real Noodle, standing on a table with a birthday cake, surrounded by children. The copy is inscribed by both Leaf and Bemelmans with an additional Bemelmans drawing of Noodle.

32.   Munro Leaf, *Noodle,* illus. Bemelmans (New York: Four Winds Press, 1969); book jacket.

33.   "Noodle" (cartoon), *Saturday Evening Post,* 29 April 1933, 22.

34.   "Bemelmans Plans New 'Best-Seller,'" *New York Times,* 14 July 1937, 19 (hereafter cited in text); "Illustrator: Man about Town Tries His Hand at Many Trades," 21.

35.   Message in Viking file, dated received 9 September 1937.

36.   Letter to Massee, 31 May 1938.

37.   Letter to Massee, undated [May 1937?], from *Santa Clara* in Bonaventura, Colombia.

38.   Letter to Massee, 4 May 1937.

39.   "The Humor of Ludwig Bemelmans," *Publishers Weekly,* 22 October 1938, 1508.

40.   The *New York Times*'s spelling of the Otovallo Indians and Bemelmans's spelling of the town of Otavalo differ.

41.   *Quito Express* (New York: Viking, 1938), 7; hereafter cited in text.

42.   Anne T. Eaton, "Mr. Bemelmans Again," *New York Times Book Review,* 30 October 1938, 12.

43.   "The Painted Grapes" (caption), *Town and Country,* September 1940, 56.

44.   May Lamberton Becker, review of *Quito Express, New York Herald Tribune Books,* 23 October 1938, 8.

45.   Louise Seaman Bechtel, review of *Quito Express, Saturday Review of Literature,* 19 November 1938, 18.

46.   "Christmas Children's Books," *New Yorker,* 3 December 1938, 62.

Chapter Three

1.   *Madeline* (New York: New Viking Edition, 1960), unpaged; all quotations are from this edition.

2.   Madeleine Bemelmans, letter to author, 26 January 1990.

3.   "The Isle of God," in *The World of Bemelmans: An Omnibus by Ludwig Bemelmans* (New York: Viking, 1955), 161. A shorter version of "The Isle of God" containing no mention of the accident or its aftermath appeared in "Our Footloose Correspondent" in the *New Yorker,* 5 August 1939, 46–47. Less than a month later, the version cited here appeared in *Small Beer,* published 28 August 1939. *Small Beer* is one of the books included in *The World of Bemelmans: An Omnibus by Ludwig Bemelmans.*

4.   "Speaking of Pictures: This Is the Story of Madeline and Her Appendix," *Life,* 4 September 1939, 6–9; hereafter cited in text.

5.   Letter to Dr. Irv Kerlan (misspelled "Ferlan"), 22 March 1947.

6.   Madeleine Bemelmans, letter to author, 31 July 1988; hereafter cited in text.

7.   Letter to Massee, 25 December 1937; hereafter cited in text.

8. Letter to Massee, received 15 December 1938; hereafter cited in text.

9. "The Isle of God (or Madeline's Origin)," in *Tell Them*, 166.

10. "And There Your Madeline Was Born," *Young Wings,* August 1953, 13; hereafter cited in text.

11. Postcard to Massee, 2 October 1958.

12. May Lamberton Becker, review of *Madeline, New York Herald Tribune Books,* 12 November 1939, 14.

13. Anne T. Eaton, "Charm in Paris," *New York Times Book Review,* 24 September 1939, 12.

14. Josephine Smith, review of *Madeline, Junior Libraries* (an appendix to *Library Journal*) 64, no. 19 (November 1939): 848.

15. *Madeline* (New York: Simon & Schuster, 1939), dust jacket.

16. Madeleine Bemelmans in a letter to the author (5 September 1994) notes that "to the best of my knowledge" Miss Clavel was a German woman who had been a governess in England, that she was not a member of a religious order, that Bemelmans "did not use her as a model but merely liked the sound of her name"; hereafter cited in text.

17. Quoted in Hermann Weyl, *Symmetry* (Princeton, N.J.: Princeton University Press, 1952), 16.

18. For a fuller discussion of symmetry and esthetic distancing in *Madeline,* see my article "Aesthetic Distancing in Ludwig Bemelmans' *Madeline,*" in *Children's Literature* (New Haven: Yale University Press, 1991), 75–89.

19. A copy of *Madeline* that Bemelmans dedicated to a young admirer (and that is now in the Anne Carroll Moore Collection at the New York Public Library, Donnell branch) bears a grim reminder of this fact: "For Sylvia Ann with every good wish for her future and for a happy and a peaceful visit to this lovely city after the Nazis are chased—Ludwig Bemelmans."

20. Edward Koren, "Miss Clavel Has a Cold," *New York Times Book Review,* 10 November 1985, 35.

21. "The Talk of the Town," *New Yorker,* 9 September 1939, 9.

22. "Ah, Paris!" *Vogue,* 15 October 1938, 68–69.

23. Lee Miller, "Paris Is Free . . . Cables Its Joy," *Vogue,* 1 October 1945, 148.

24. Raoul Dufy, covers for *Town and Country* for January, February, and May, 1937. Bemelmans did *Town and Country* covers for January 1938 ("Winter on the Arlberg"), February 1940 (a hotel scene), February 1942 (a ski scene), June 1942 (war scene), February 1951 (New York in snow), and December 1960 (Christmas).

25. Introduction, dated 13 July 1959, to *Bemelmans' New York* catalog.

26. "*Trompe l'oeil* Decor," *Vogue,* 15 February 1939, 50–53.

27. Angelica Zander Rudenstine, "Pablo Ruiz Picasso: *Verre et bouteille de Bass,*" in *Modern Painting, Drawing, and Sculpture Collected by Emily and Joseph*

Pulitzer, Jr., vol. 4 (Cambridge: Harvard University Art Museums, 1988), 809–15.

28. *Vogue,* 1 April 1942, 60–61, and *House and Garden,* August 1942, 21.

29. Felicity Barringer, "Stuff Misty for Me, and Other Tales of Growing Up," *New York Times Book Review,* 16 May 1993, 30.

30. "The Story of Bemelmans' *Madeline," Publishers Weekly,* 14 November 1960, 17; hereafter cited in text.

31. "Madeline at the Coronation," *Collier's,* 6 June 1953, 18–19.

32. *Madeline's Rescue* (New York: Viking, 1953); hereafter cited in text as *MR.*

33. "#13, Rue St. Augustin," *Town and Country,* May 1947, 88.

34. Lyn Ellen Lacy, *Art and Design in Children's Picture Books: An Analysis of Caldecott Award–Winning Illustrations* (Chicago and London: American Library Association, 1986), 99.

35. On the use of visual metonyms as a cue to a character's status, see William Moebius's "Introduction to Picturebook Codes," *Word and Image* (April–June 1986): 141–58.

36. Henri Bergson, *Laughter* (1900), in *Comedy,* translated by arrangement with Presses Universitaires de France (Garden City, N.Y.: Doubleday Anchor, 1956), 94–95.

37. Shelton L. Root, Jr., "Ludwig Bemelmans and His Books for Children," *Elementary English* 36, no. 1 (January 1957): 10.

38. "Bemelmans," Hammer Galleries exhibition brochure, 20 November to 22 December 1956.

39. "Author-Artist," 6; found in the Bemelmans clipping file of the New York Public Library, Donnell branch; hereafter cited in the text. Possibly M. S. Libby, review of *Madeline and the Bad Hat, New York Herald Tribune Books,* 12 May 1957, 6.

40. "Poor Animal!" *Globe,* December 1937–January 1938, 25–27; reprinted in *The Donkey Inside* (New York: Viking, 1944), 169–73.

41. "Speaking Out against Vivisection," *Town and Country,* December 1962, 141.

42. Letter to Massee, 23 June 1956; hereafter cited in text.

43. *Madeline and the Bad Hat* (New York: Viking, 1957), 19; hereafter cited in text as *MBH.*

44. See Rene Huyghe, "Color and the Expression of Interior Time in Western Art," *Color Symbolism: Six Excerpts from the Eranos Yearbook 1972* (Dallas: Spring Publications, 1977), 143.

45. *Madeline and the Gypsies* (New York: Viking, 1959), 56; hereafter cited in text as *MG.*

46. "Madeline and the Gypsies," *McCall's,* December 1958, unpaged insert; hereafter cited in text.

47. "Madeline in London," *Holiday,* August 1961, 50–55.

48. Letter to Massee, 11 October 1960; hereafter cited in text.

49. *Madeline in London* (New York: Viking, 1961), 54–55; hereafter cited in text as *ML.*

50. Letter to "Marcel," 29 October 1960; hereafter cited in text. I am assuming that the "Marcel" he writes to here and "Marcel Salinas" are the same person, the assistant he refers to in his 30 November 1960 letter to Claridge's.

51. Letter to Lord Edward Stanley, London, 29 October 1960.

52. Letter in Viking file, almost certainly to Massee, 13 January 1961; hereafter cited in text.

53. To Viking, 4 March 1961.

54. Letter to Massee, 29 November 1960.

55. Letter to Claridge's, 30 November 1960.

56. Letter to Jeanine de Goldschmidt Rothschild in Paris, 30 October 1960. He asks her to ship the originals back to the Hammer Galleries.

57. Letter to Massee, 2 May 1961.

58. Letter to Massee, no date, probably May 1961.

59. Letter to Massee, 15 May 1961.

60. Letter to "Annis" at Viking, 7 July 1961. I suspect this is the "a.j.d." of an in-house memo of 24 May. Bemelmans had written to "Annis" earlier about text changes, placement, and images for the back cover and subtitle page. Someone else at Viking identified as "m.a.b." [Marshall?] also made suggestions to Bemelmans about rhymes in a letter to him of 15 May 1961.

61. Letter to Massee, 29 March 1961.

62. Donnarae MacCann and Olga Richards, *The Child's First Books: A Critical Study of Pictures and Text* (New York: H. W. Wilson, 1973), 116–17.

63 Letter to Massee, 16 March 1961.

64. Letter to Massee, 23 June 1956; hereafter cited in text.

65. Letter to Massee, 27 June 1956; hereafter cited in text.

66. "Madeline's Christmas," *McCall's,* December 1956, unpaged insert.

67. *Madeline's Christmas* (New York: Viking, 1985), unpaged; all quotations are from this edition.

68. Letter to Massee, 20 July 1962; hereafter cited in text.

69. "Bemelmans," Hammer Galleries exhibition brochure, 22 November to 22 December 1956. Originals of *Madeline and the Bad Hat* and *Madeline's Christmas.*

70. Bemelmans's original draft read, "And everyone from Istanbul to the Panamanian Isthmus—Was suddenly whisked home for Christmas" (27 June 1956). On Viking memo paper, a hand other than Bemelmans's introduced a version somewhat closer to the lines that finally appeared.

71. "Madeline's Christmas," *McCall's,* December 1985, 112–17.

72. *Madeline* (New York: Simon & Schuster, 1954), Little Golden Book Edition.

73. "Madeline's Christmas," *Good Housekeeping,* December 1955, 74–79; hereafter cited in text.

74. *Madeline's Christmas in Texas* (New York 1955), unpaged; hereafter cited in text.

75. In a telephone interview (January 1989), Jane Rohlfing of the Special Collections Department of the University of Colorado at Boulder described the book to me.

76. "Big Hats for Little Girls," Rochester, N.Y., *Democrat Chronicle* magazine, *New York This Week,* 22 March 1959, 27.

Chapter Four

1. *Fifi* (New York: Simon & Schuster, 1940), unpaged; all quotations are from this edition.

2. "Fifi," *Town and Country,* August 1940, 29–32.

3. *Rosebud* (New York: Random House, 1942): dust jacket; hereafter cited in text as *R.*

4. Ellen Lewis Buell, "The Tricky Rabbit," *New York Times Book Review,* 4 October 1942, 35.

5. "Nosegay," *Town and Country,* April 1942, 42–43.

6. Madeleine Bemelmans, letter to author, 31 July 1988.

7. Letter to Massee, stamped 20 June 1941.

8. *Fiction, Folklore, Fantasy, and Poetry for Children, 1876–1985* (New York: R. R. Bowker, 1986) lists *A Tale of Two Glimps.*

9. *A Tale of Two Glimps* (New York: CBS, 1947), unpaged; all quotations are from this edition.

10. Letter to Massee, 1 November 1949; hereafter cited in text.

11. *Sunshine: A Story about the City of New York* (New York: Simon & Schuster, 1950), unpaged; all quotations are from this edition.

12. See Virginia Kirkus's *Bookshop Service* 18, no. 9 (1 May 1950): 260. See also the *Bulletin of the Children's Book Center* 3, no. 7 (June 1950): 44.

13. "The Happy Place," *Woman's Home Companion,* April 1951, 28–31[+]; hereafter cited in text.

14. *The Happy Place* (Boston: Little, Brown,1952); hereafter cited in text as *HP.*

15. *The High World* (New York: Harper & Brothers, 1954); hereafter cited in text as *HW.*

16. Letter to Massee, 6 April 1948.

17. Clipping enclosed with letter; unnamed newspaper.

18. The second Republic of Austria was established after Germany's defeat in 1945. Democracy was not well established in Austria at the time of Bemelmans's 1948 letter from Lech am Arlberg.

19.   Elizabeth A. Groves, review of *The High World, Saturday Review,* 13 November 1954, 76, and Louise S. Bechtel, review of *The High World, New York Herald Tribune Books,* 14 November 1954, 2.

20.   "The Old Stag and the Tree," *Woman's Day,* January 1954, 20.

21.   *Parsley* (New York: Harper & Row, 1955); hereafter cited in text as *P.*

22.   Hammer Galleries exhibition brochure, 30 November and 31 December; probably in 1955, shortly after the book's appearance.

23.   Review of *Parsley, Bulletin of the Children's Book Center* 9, no. 6 (February 1956): 66.

24.   Madeleine Bemelmans, letter to author, 5 September 1994. The Beverley Bogert in question is seemingly the New York banker and sportsman (1868–1959) described in *The National Encyclopaedia of American Biography,* 50–51. "Randy" and *Welcome Home!* were published in the year after Bogert's death.

25.   "Randy," *Mademoiselle,* December 1959, 42–45.

26.   *Welcome Home!* after a poem by Beverley Bogert (New York: Harper & Bros, 1960), unpaged; all quotations are from this edition.

27.   "Bemelmans: Recent Paintings," Hammer Galleries exhibition brochure, 1–24 December 1960.

28.   *Marina* (New York: Harper & Row, 1962), unpaged; all quotations are from this edition.

29.   "Noodles: The Trained Seal" (cartoon), *Saturday Evening Post,* 29 April 1933, 22.

Chapter Five

1.   *Madeline: A Pop-Up Book Based on the Original* (New York: Viking Kestrel, 1987).

2.   *Madeline's House* (New York: Viking Penguin, 1989).

3.   *Mad about Madeline* (New York: Viking, 1993).

4.   *Madeleine* (Paris: Lutin poche de l'école des loisirs, 1985), 40.

5.   "Smithsonian Gift Catalogue," Spring 1988.

6.   "Viking to Issue Lost Madeline by Bemelmans," *Publishers Weekly,* 19 July 1985, 32.

7.   Zohar Shavit, *Poetics of Children's Literature* (Athens: University of Georgia Press, 1986), 69; hereafter cited in text.

8.   I am also indebted to Michael Patrick Hearne for introducing these concepts in a class at Columbia University.

9.   Anne Carroll Moore, "A List of Books Recommended for a Children's Library" (Iowa Library Commission, 1905?), 4; cited in Bader, 7.

10.   Ruth K. MacDonald, *Dr. Seuss* (Boston: Twayne Publishers, 1988), 6.

11.   See, for instance, Margret and H. A. Rey, "Zozo," on "A Page for Children," *Good Housekeeping,* July 1951, 126.

12.   Bernard Wiseman, telephone interview, 20 January 1992.

13.   Selma G. Lanes, *The Art of Maurice Sendak* (New York: Harry N. Abrams, 1980), 9.

14.   Patricia Dooley, "The Window in the Book: Conventions in the Illustration of Children's Books," *Wilson Library Bulletin* (October 1980): 108–12.

15.   Peggy Whalen-Levitt, "Breaking Frame: Bordering on Illusion," *School Library Journal* (March 1986): 100–103.

16.   Linda Kauffman Peterson and Marilyn Leathers Solt, *Newbery and Caldecott Medal and Honor Books: An Annotated Bibliography* (Boston: G. K. Hall, 1982), 244; hereafter cited in text.

17.   May Lamberton Becker, review of *Madeline, New York Herald Tribune Books,* 12 November 1939, 14.

18.   "Marshall, James (Edward)," in *Something about the Author,* vol. 51, ed. Anne Commire (Detroit: Gale Research, 1988), 120.

19.   Review of *The Purple Coat, Kirkus Reviews,* 15 August 1986, 1291.

20.   Madeleine Bemelmans, letter to author, 31 July 1988.

21.   Jim Trelease, *The New Read-Aloud Handbook,* rev. ed. (New York: Viking Penguin, 1989), 180.

22.   Bernice E. Cullinan, *Literature and the Child,* 2d ed. (San Diego: Harcourt Brace Jovanovich, 1989), 196.

23.   Judy Blume, "Friends for Life," *Once Upon a Time* (New York: G. P. Putnam's Sons, 1986), 24–25.

Selected Bibliography

PRIMARY WORKS

Children's Books: Author and Illustrator

The Castle Number Nine. New York: Viking, 1937.

Fifi. New York: Simon & Schuster, 1940. Originally published in *Town and Country,* August 1940, 29–32.

The Golden Basket. New York: Viking, 1936.

Hansi. New York: Viking, 1934.

The Happy Place. Boston: Little, Brown, 1952. Originally published in *Woman's Home Companion,* April 1951, 28–31+.

The High World. New York: Harper, 1954. Originally published as "Christmas in Tyrol." *Holiday,* December 1950, 64–65, 67+.

Mad about Madeline: The Complete Tales. Introduction by Anna Quindlen. New York: Viking, 1993.

Madeleine. Paris: L'école des loisirs, 1985. Unlike the original, this version has the correct number of little girls at the table in the final scene.

Madeline. New York: Simon & Schuster, 1939; New York: Viking, 1958; New York: New Viking Edition, 1960. Originally published as "Speaking of Pictures: This Is the Story of Madeline and Her Appendix." *Life,* 4 September 1939, 6–9.

Madeline. Little Golden Book. New York: Simon & Schuster, 1954.

Madeline and the Bad Hat. New York: Viking, 1957.

Madeline and the Gypsies. New York: Viking, 1959. Originally published in *McCall's,* December 1958, insert.

Madeline in London. New York: Viking, 1961. Originally published in *Holiday,* August 1961, 50–55.

Madeline's Christmas. New York: Viking, 1985. Originally published in *McCall's,* December 1956, insert. Also in *McCall's,* December 1985, 112–17.

Madeline's Christmas in Texas. Neiman Marcus, 1955. Originally published as "Madeline's Christmas." *Good Housekeeping,* December 1955, 74–79. Copy located in the Rare Books Room, University of Colorado, Boulder, library.

Madeline's Rescue. New York: Viking, 1953. Originally published in *Good Housekeeping,* December 1951, 55–60.

Marina. New York: Harper, 1962.

Parsley. New York: Harper, 1955. Originally published as "The Old Stag and the Tree." *Woman's Day,* January 1954, 20.

Quito Express. New York: Viking, 1938.

Rosebud. New York: Random House, 1942; New York: Knopf, 1993. Originally published as "Nosegay." *Town and Country,* April 1942, 42–43.

Sunshine: A Story about the City of New York. New York: Simon & Schuster, 1950. Originally published as "Sunshine, Sunshine Go Away." *Good Housekeeping,* December 1949, 63–76.

A Tale of Two Glimps. New York: CBS, 1947.

Welcome Home! New York: Harper, 1960. Originally published as "Randy." *Mademoiselle,* December 1959, 42–45.

Children's Book Illustrator

Leaf, Munro. *Noodle.* New York: F. A. Stokes, 1937; New York: Four Winds Press, 1969.

Comic Strips

"Noodles, the Trained Seal." The *Saturday Evening Post,* 29 April 1933, 22.

"Silly Willy, the Trained Seal." *Young America* (New York), edited by Stuart Scheftel, 8 March 1935 to ca. 1937.

"Thrilling Adventures of Count Bric a Brac." *New York World*'s *World Magazine,* 4 July 1926 to ca. 1927; *Milwaukee Journal,* 19 September to 12 December 1926.

Adult Novels

Are You Hungry Are You Cold. Cleveland: World, 1960.

The Blue Danube. New York: Viking, 1945.

Dirty Eddie. New York: Viking, 1947.

The Eye of God. New York: Viking, 1949.

Now I Lay Me Down To Sleep. New York: Viking, 1944.

The Street Where the Heart Lies. Cleveland: World, 1962; New York: Heineman, 1993.

The Woman of My Life. New York: Viking, 1957.

Other Works

"Ah, Paris!" *Vogue,* 15 October 1938, 68–69. Humorous insights into Parisian life presented in cartoon scenes, published the year before *Madeline.*

"And There Your *Madeline* Was Born." *Young Wings,* August 1953, 12–13. This account of the inspiration for *Madeline's Rescue,* targeted to young readers, varies in several particulars from that given in the Caldecott Acceptance Award.

"Art at the Hotel Splendide." *New Yorker,* 1 June 1940, 28–32. As a young waiter at the Splendide hotel, Bemelmans learns cartooning by drawing the clients on the backs of menus. In *Hotel Bemelmans* as "Art at the

Splendide," 63–71. New York: Viking, 1946. Also in *La Bonne Table,* 65–72. New York: Simon & Schuster, 1964.

"Art Class." Frustrating lessons in New York with Thaddeus. In *Tell Them It Was Wonderful,* ed. Madeleine Bemelmans, 65–66. New York: Viking, 1985. Originally part of "Life Class." In *Life Class,* 89–100. New York: Viking, 1938.

"Art for Art's Sake." *Town and Country,* July 1945, 54–55[+]. Gives his impressions of a year in Hollywood, where he had been working on *Yolanda and the Thief.* Describes himself as "not a writer but a graphic workman," moving from image to image.

At Your Service. Way of Life Series. Evanston, Ill.: Row, Peterson, 1941.

Bemelmans' Italian Holiday. Foreword by Ted Patrick. Boston: Houghton Mifflin, 1961.

Bemelmans' New York. Introduction to an exhibition of paintings by Ludwig Bemelmans. New York: Museum of the City of New York, 1959. Discusses his appreciation of artwork by children.

The Best of Times: An Account of Europe Revisited. New York: Simon & Schuster, 1948.

La Bonne Table. Selected and edited by Donald and Eleanor Friede. New York: Simon & Schuster, 1964; Boston: David R. Godine, 1989.

"Caldecott Award Acceptance Paper." *Horn Book* 30 (August 1954): 270–75.

"The Count and the Cobbler." *Harper's Bazaar,* December 1935, 52–53. A Christmas story consisting of 21 illustrations and unrhymed text in which the cobbler's baby cleverly designs shoes for the entire family.

"Dear General—What a Surprise!" *Town and Country,* August 1939, 30–31[+]. Hilarious account of his failed efforts as an actor in *Good Hunting: A Satire in Three Acts.* In *Small Beer,* 147–68. New York: Viking, 1939.

The Donkey Inside. New York: Viking, 1941; New York: Paragon House Publishers, 1990.

Father, Dear Father. New York: Viking, 1953; New York: Heineman, 1992.

"A Gemütliche Christmas." *Town and Country,* December 1957, 79–80. After sharing a Depression-era Christmas with German friends, Bemelmans mails a sketch of one of them to the *Saturday Evening Post,* where it is accepted. Excerpted and amended in "The Old Ritz," in *Tell Them It was Wonderful,* ed. Madeleine Bemelmans, 156–62. New York: Viking, 1985.

Holiday in France. Essays collected and illustrated and with an Introduction by Bemelmans. Boston: Houghton Mifflin, 1957.

Hotel Bemelmans. New York: Viking, 1946.

Hotel Splendide. New York: Viking, 1941; Mattituck, N.Y.: Amereon, n.d.; New York: Heinemann, 1993.

How To Have Europe All to Yourself. European Travel Commission, 1960.

How To Travel Incognito. Boston: Little, Brown, 1952; New York: Heineman, 1992.

I Love You, I Love You, I Love You. New York: Viking, 1942; New York: Heineman, 1992.

"The Isle of God." In *Small Beer,* 113–32. New York: Viking, 1939. This sketch of a vacation off the coast of France ends in a biking accident and a trip to the hospital where there is a little appendectomy patient in a room nearby. A much shorter piece entitled "The Isle of God"—not mentioning either the accident or the hospital—appeared less than a month earlier in the *New Yorker,* 4 August 1939, 46–47.

"The Isle of God (or Madeline's Origin)." In *Tell Them It Was Wonderful,* 163–66. New York: Viking, 1985. At some time after the publication of *Madeline's Rescue,* Bemelmans added three paragraphs to the story of his accident and hospital stay as it had first appeared in "The Isle of God" in *Small Beer.*

Life Class. New York: Viking, 1938.

"Ludwig Bemelmans' Splendide Apartment." *Vogue,* 1 April 1942, 60–61⁺. Bemelmans describes and draws the eclectic furnishings and decor of his new Gramercy Park apartment.

Mad about Madeline: The Complete Tales. Introduction by Anna Quindlen. New York: Viking, 1993. Also in *Mad about Madeline:* rare photos of Bemelmans with wife Madeleine and daughter Barbara dated 1940–41, sketches for the *Madeline* books, and "The Isle of God (or Madeline's Origin), 313–20.

"Madeline at the Coronation." *Collier's,* 6 June 1953, 18–19. To see the coronation of Elizabeth II, Madeline and her entourage travel to England and back again in nine full-color illustrations with rhyming text.

"May Massee as Her Author-Illustrators See Her." *Horn Book* 12 (July–August 1936): 231. Reflects on how the "brave lady" dealt with a manuscript for *Hansi* written on odd scraps of paper and pictures "either too big or too small and never finished on time."

"Monsieur Carnewal and the Start of the Story." In *Writing Books for Boys and Girls: A Young Wings Anthology of Essays by Two Hundred Sixteen Authors Who Tell How They Came To Write Their Special Kinds of Books for Young Readers,* edited by Helen Ferris, 85–87. Garden City, N.Y.: Junior Literary Guild/Doubleday, 1952. His Gmunden childhood as reflected in *The Golden Basket.*

My Life in Art. New York: Harper, 1958. Includes "Swan Country" and other essays and full-page color paintings.

My War with the United States. New York: Viking, 1937.

"The Old Ritz." In *Tell Them It Was Wonderful,* ed. Madeleine Bemelmans, 157–62. New York: Viking, 1985. Describes early days as a cartoonist, leaving the hotel business, and meeting Massee. A portion appeared in "A Gemütliche Christmas." *Town and Country,* December 1957, 79–80⁺.

On Board Noah's Ark. New York: Viking, 1962.

"Speaking Out against Vivisection." *Town and Country,* December 1962, 141. Reprint of drawing Bemelmans made for the Vivisection Investigation League.

Small Beer. New York: Viking, 1939.

"Swan Country." In *My Life in Art,* 7–22. New York: Harper, 1958. Poignant memories of Bemelmans's childhood in Gmunden followed by an account of how he began to paint in oils in 1953. A version with only minor changes, entitled "When You Lunch with the Emperor," appeared shortly before the book's publication in *Vogue*, 1 September 1958, 208–9+. "Swan Country" also appears in *Tell Them It Was Wonderful*, ed. Madeleine Bemelmans, 3–11. New York: Viking, 1985. This version omits Bemelmans's account of his return to oil painting, but several paragraphs have been added in which he describes boyhood memories of his mother.

Tell Them It Was Wonderful: Selected Writings by Ludwig Bemelmans, ed. Madeleine Bemelmans. Introduction by Madeleine Bemelmans; foreword by Norman Cousins. New York: Viking, 1985. Chronologically arranged compilation of some of Bemelmans's best autobiographical writings, some of which have been excerpted and rearranged.

To the One I Love the Best. New York: Viking, 1955.

"A Trip to Bruges." *Vogue*, September 1936, 88–89. This illustrated travel article presents many of the subjects treated in *The Golden Basket*, including schoolgirls walking in rows.

"When You Lunch with the Emperor." *Vogue*, 1 September 1958, 208–9+. Earliest version of "Swan Country," which appeared two months later in *My Life in Art*, 7–23. New York: Harper, 1958.

The World of Bemelmans: An Omnibus by Ludwig Bemelmans. New York: Viking, 1955. Contains *My War with the United States; Small Beer; The Donkey Inside; I Love You, I Love You, I Love You;* and five new stories.

SECONDARY WORKS

Articles and Parts of Books

Bader, Barbara. "Ludwig Bemelmans." In *American Picturebooks: From Noah's Ark to the Beast Within*, 47–51. New York: Macmillan, 1976. Bader's treatment of Bemelmans's early books includes histories of the books' making along with valuable critical perspectives on art and design. Particularly appreciates *The Castle Number Nine* and *Madeline*.

Barringer, Felicity. "Stuff Misty for Me, and Other Tales of Growing Up." *New York Times Book Review*, 16 May 1993, 30. Includes a brief interview with grown-up Barbara Bemelmans Marciano about her relationship to Madeline.

Eastman, Jacqueline F. "Aesthetic Distancing in Ludwig Bemelmans' *Madeline*." In *Children's Literature*, 75–89. New Haven: Yale University Press, 1991. The many aspects of *Madeline* that signal that the work is art, and not reality, permit a young reader to enjoy danger at a safe emotional distance. The striking symmetry of plot and images in itself offers a sense of security.

Groff, Patrick. "The Children's World of Ludwig Bemelmans." *Elementary English* 43, no. 6 (October 1966): 559–68. Discusses how Bemelmans's visual art appeals to the child reader.

Heins, Ethel. "Ludwig Bemelmans." *Writers for Children: Critical Studies of Major Authors since the Seventeenth Century*, edited by Jane M. Bingham, 55–61.

New York: Scribners, 1988. Insightful analysis of Bemelmans's works for children, omitting only the uncanonized *Tale of Two Glimps* and *Madeline's Christmas in Texas.*

"Home Splendide." *House and Garden,* August 1942, 20–21. Text and photographs of Bemelmans, Mimi, and Barbara in their uniquely furnished New York apartment.

"The Humor of Ludwig Bemelmans." *Publishers Weekly,* 22 October 1938, 1508–10. A good summary of Bemelmans's career up through *Quito Express.* Notes that his imagination turns the real world "slightly fantastic," a quality pleasing to both adults and children.

"Illustrator: Man about Town Tries His Hand at Many Trades." *Newsweek,* 24 July 1937, 21. Biographical sketch early in his career when Bemelmans had just returned from Ecuador brimming with ideas. Mentions "Count Bric a Brac." Includes photo of Bemelmans sketching and typing in his bathtub.

Lacy, Lyn Ellen. *Art and Design in Children's Picture Books: An Analysis of Caldecott Award–Winning Illustrations,* 98–100. Chicago: American Library Association, 1986. Points to a Fauvist influence in Bemelmans's use of color in *Madeline's Rescue.*

MacCann, Donnarae, and Olga Richard. "Outstanding Contemporary Illustrators: Ludwig Bemelmans (1898–62)" and "The Caldecott Award." In *The Child's First Books: A Critical Study of Pictures and Texts,* 47–48, 115–20. New York: Wilson, 1973. Discusses Bemelmans's use of the "twelve little girls" as a design motif, his ability to convey movement, and to present architecture through a style similar to that of the Dufy brothers. Regrets the lack of Caldecott attention to *Madeline in London.*

"Madeline's Master." *Newsweek,* 15 October 1962, 115. This obituary first quotes Bemelmans's exaggerated statement that *Madeline* went unpublished for five years.

Massee, May. "Ludwig Bemelmans." *Horn Book* 30 (August 1954): 263–69. Bemelmans's Viking editor looks back at his career, quoting extensively from two of his autobiographical Viking publications for adults, *My War with the United States* and *Father, Dear Father.*

Massee, May. "Caldecott Award to Bemelmans." *Library Journal* 79 (15 March 1954): 484–85. Massee offers impressions of Bemelmans from their first meeting to 1954, commenting particularly on the creation of *Hansi.*

"People Watcher." *Time,* 31 March 1952, 74. At a Houston gallery opening of his work, Bemelmans comments on the fun of painting—and the fun of selling.

Peterson, Linda Kauffman, and Marilyn Leathers Solt. *Newbery and Caldecott Medal and Honor Books: An Annotated Bibliography,* 244, 297–98. Boston: G. K. Hall, 1982. Short plot summaries and analytical remarks. Finds the energy of *Madeline's* text and illustrations to be unique among early winners.

Pitz, Henry C. "Ludwig Bemelmans." *American Artist* 15 (May 1951): 48–49. Shows Bemelmans to be a citizen of the world, moving amongst his

dwellings, entertaining lavishly. Notes that his drawings have a unique
ability to convey "the little sidelights of the human heart."

Powers, W. A. "My Friend Ludwig." *Town and Country,* December 1962,
128–33⁺. Affectionately describes Bemelmans's working relationship
with a longtime editor at the magazine; many photos.

Rogow, Lee. "A Younger Bemelmaniac." *Saturday Review,* August 1953, 13–14.
Reviewing both *Father, Dear Father* and *Madeline's Rescue,* Rogow notes
similarities in the settings and inhabitants of Bemelmans's fictional
world, which he coins "Bemelmania." An interview by Bernard Kalb with
13-year-old Barbara is included.

Root, Shelton L., Jr. "Ludwig Bemelmans and His Books for Children."
Elementary English 36 (January 1957): 3–12. Discusses books through
Madeline and the Bad Hat. Finds *Hansi* to be Bemelmans's best and rec-
ommends reading it aloud, a bit at a time. Criticizes the plot of *Madeline's
Rescue* and finds *Parsley* lacking in imagination.

"Speaking of Pictures: This Is the Story of Madeline and Her Appendix." *Life,*
4 September 1939, 6–9. Beside pictures and text outlining the imminent
publication, this article includes brief background information on
Madeline's inspiration and a picture of Barbara on a donkey.

"The Story of Bemelmans' *Madeline.*" *Publishers Weekly,* 14 November 1960,
16–17. Published sometime after the appearance of *Madeline and the
Gypsies,* this article relates well-known information about the history of
the *Madeline* books as well as details about sales, other editions, magazine
versions, television programs, movies, and a record.

Van Gelder, Robert. "An Interview with Ludwig Bemelmans." *New York Times
Book Review,* 26 January 1941, 2⁺. Bemelmans describes the incident that
caused him to emigrate to America and gives insights into his work
habits and lifestyle.

Bibliography

Pomerance, Murray, ed. and comp. *Ludwig Bemelmans: A Bibliography.* New
York: James H. Heineman, 1993. This valuable product of 10 years of
research, nearly 400 pages long, is a first and magnificent attempt to catalog everything written by or about Bemelmans in many languages.

Catalog

Hodowanec, George V., ed. *The May Massee Collection: Creative Publishing for
Children, 1923–1963: A Checklist.* Emporia, Kans.: Emporia State
University, 1979. The relatively limited Bemelmans collection includes
several pieces of original book artwork. I believe I have clarified that one
letter cataloged under *Castle Number Nine* refers instead to *My War with
the United States*.

Index

Abrams, Lester, 120
Alfred A. Knopf, 94
Ardizzone, Edward, 119
Are You Hungry Are You Cold, 7
Artzybasheff, Boris, 24, 55
Astaire, Fred, 5
At Your Service: The Way of Life in a Hotel, 6

Bader, Barbara, 24, 29, 39, 59, 61–62, 68, 118
Bechtel, Louise Seaman, 49
Becker, May Lamberton, 48–49, 53, 54, 120
Bemelmans, Barbara, 3, 9, 61–62, 85, 126n14; *Father, Dear Father* and, 7, 8, 10, 11, 103, 143
Bemelmans, Frances Fischer, 1
Bemelmans, Lambert, 1
Bemelmans, Ludwig: cartooning, 21–23, 42–43, 59–60; childhood and education of, 1–2, 24; children's books of, 13–16; as comic strip artist, 2–3, 3–4, 16–19; death of, 7; development as an author/artist, 10–13; early career of, 2–3; exhibition and sale of paintings of, 6–7, 8, 69, 84, 100, 107, 112–13; as "graphic workman," 11, 16, 21; houses owned by, 9–10; immigration to America, 2; last years of career of, 6–7; marriage of, 3; meeting with Massee of, 3, 9, 20–21, 125n13; new creative outlets in the 1940s for, 5–6; "no imagination," 12–13; novels of, 7; personality and working habits of, 7–8; preference for painting by, 10, 11, 21; research used by, 12, 77–78; rise to fame in the 1930s, 3–5; sense of security in home as theme of, 9–10, 25–26, 31, 55–56; theater work of, 4–5, 27; visual memory of, 11–12
Bemelmans, Madeleine (Mimi) Freund, 9, 27, 43, 69; dedication of *Madeline and*

the Bad Hat to, 69; letters to author from, xi, 17, 51, 51–52, 61, 65, 66, 69, 85, 92, 121, 131n16, 135n24; marriage of, 3; on Bemelmans's tastes and work, xi, 17, 51–52, 65, 66, 69, 85, 92, 121, 131n16, 135n24; writings by, 1–2, 7, 125n3, 126n14, 129n19
Bemelmans Bar, Hotel Carlyle, New York, 9
Bergson, Henri, 66
Berndt, Walter, 16
Berry, Erick, 25
Best of Times: An Account of Europe Revisited, 6
Bishop, Claire, 55
Blackbeard, Bill, x, 3, 16, 18
Blue Danube, The, 5–6
Blum, Léon, 51, 55–56
Blume, Judy, 123
Bogert, Beverley, 10, 110, 135n24
Braques, Georges, 66
Bremer, Lucille, 5
Burgess, Thornton, 16
Burton, Virginia Lee, 121
Busch, Wilhelm, 17–18, 55, 124

Caldecott Award, 119, 120, 121, 122, 124; *see also Madeline's Rescue*
Caldecott Committee. *See Madeline in London*
Caldecott Honor Award, 119, 120, 121, 122, 124; *see also Madeline*
Castle Number Nine, The, 3, 10, 15, 36–43; Bemelmans on, 97; caricature in, 18; drawing from, 37 (illus.); folk tale parody in, 37–39; illustrations in, 39–40, 93; norms of juvenile publishing in, 15, 42; plot of, 13, 36–37; published antecedent to, 40–41; reception for, 41–43
CBS. *See* Columbia Broadcasting System
Children's Literature Association, 119

145

"Christmas in Tyrol," 15, 102
Citizen Kane (film), 92
Collier's (magazine), 63
Columbia Broadcasting System (CBS), 5, 94
"Count and the Cobbler, The" 21, 40
"Count Bric a Brac." *See* "Thrilling Adventures of Count Bric a Brac"
Cousins, Norman, 8
Crespi, Marc Antonio, 69
Cronyn, Hume, 5
Cullinan, Bernice, 122, 124

d'Aulaire, Ingri, and Edgar Parin, 24, 105, 120, 121
de Angeli, Marguerite, 124
de Brunhoff, Jean, 118
Denslow, W. W., 118
Derain, André, 66
de Regniers, Beatrice Schenk, 124
de Ungerer, Tomi, 120
de Vlaminck, Maurice, 66
Dirty Eddie, 6
Disney, Walt, 119
Dr. Doolittle (Lofting), 16
Donkey Inside, The, 6, 132n40
Dooly, Patricia, 120
Dufy, Raoul, 58

Eaton, Anne T., 27, 48, 54
Egielski, Richard, 120
Eisner, Will, 17
Elizabeth II, Queen of England, 63
Eye of God, The, 6

F. A. Stokes, 20, 42, 43, 52
Father, Dear Father, 7, 8, 10, 11, 103, 106
Félix, Monique, 120
Fifi, 5, 14, 89–91; illustrations in, 90–91; narration of, 18; plot of, 13; publication of, 89, 98
Fish, Helen Dean, 120, 121
Flack, Marjorie, 26, 123
Françoise (Françoise Seignobosc), 24
Frey, Dagobert, 56
Four Winds, 44
Friede, Donald and Eleanor, 8, 27, 35

Gág, Wanda, 24, 55
Gammell, Stephen, 121
Geisel, Theodor Seuss, 119, 124
Glaser, William, 29
Glick, Milton, 93–94, 129n28
Goble, Paul, 121
Golden Basket, The, 10, 27–35, 54, 62; adult appeal of, 34–35; associations with Gmunden of, 32–34; caricature in, 18; creation of, 27–29; drawing from, 32 (illus.) ; foreign words used in, 47; illustrations in, 29, 39, 41, 60, 105; Newbery Honor Award for, 1, 3, 27, 29–31; norms of juvenile publishing in, 15, 29; plot of, 12; previews of *Madeline,* 31–32
Goodall, John S., 120
Goode, Diane, 121
Good Housekeeping (magazine), 5, 15, 63, 119; "Madeline's Christmas" in, 86–87; "Madeline's Rescue" in, 63; "Sunshine Sunshine Go Away: A Story about the City of New York" in, 96, 102
Good Hunting: A Satire in Three Acts (West and Schrank), 4–5

Hammer Galleries, 6–7, 69, 84, 107, 113
Handforth, Thomas, 25, 120, 121
Hansi, 4, 20–27, 30, 31, 54, 106; drawing from, 26 (illus.); dummies, 21–22; foreign words used in, 47; illustrations in, 8, 9–10, 29, 44, 60, 105, 118; overcoming "cartoonitis," 21–23; norms of juvenile publishing in, 15, 23–27; plot of, 12, 26; publication of, 21
Happy Place, The, 6, 99–102
Hapsburg House restaurant, 3, 9
Harper & Brothers, 102, 106, 110
Harper & Row, 113
Harper's Bazaar (magazine), 21, 40
Heins, Ethel, 10, 61, 87
High World, The, 6, 9, 10, 102–5, 106; caricature in, 18; illustrations in, 104, 105; plot of, 13, 102–3
Holiday (magazine), 7, 75, 76 (illus.), 77, 78, 82, 102, 103
Horn, Maurice, 17, 59

Hornbook (magazine), 20–21
Hotel Bemelmans, 6
Hotel Carlyle, New York, 9
Hotel Splendide, 6
House and Garden (magazine), 9
House Beautiful (magazine), 4

I Love You, I Love You, I Love You, 6
"Isle of God, The," 51
"Isle of God, The (or Madeline's Origin),"
    53

Jacobs, Joseph, 37–38
Jeffers, Susan, 124
Jersey City Printing Company, 29
Johnson, Crockett, 120
Junior Libraries (magazine), 54
Junior Literary Guild, 10, 65, 82

Katzenjammer Kids, 17, 118
Keats, Ezra Jack, 123
Kellogg, Stephen, 120
Kennedy, Caroline, 82
Kennedy, Jackie, 82
Klee, Paul, 66
Knight, Hilary, 122
Koren, Edward, 57

La Bonne Table (Friede and Friede), 27, 35
Lacy, Lyn Ellen, 66
Lathrop, Dorothy, 120, 121
"Lausbub," 2, 10, 36
Lawson, Robert, 26, 120, 121, 123
Leaf, Munro, 3, 26, 94, 123; Bemelmans's
    illustrations for, 3, 14, 20, 42, 43–45,
    92
Liddell, Mark, 3
Life (magazine), 51, 53, 57, 61
Life Class, 2, 4, 6
Little Golden Book, 86
Lobel, Arnold, 120
Lofting, Hugh, 16
Ludwig, Emil, 38–39

Macaulay, David, 120
MacCann, Donnarae, 82
Mad about Madeline, 116

Madeline, 50–62; appeals to adults in, 15,
    53–54, 57–61; Caldecott Honor Award
    for, 1, 50; cartooning approach to,
    59–61; creation of, 12; drawing from,
    60 (illus.); folk tale elements in, 54–55;
    illustrations in, 12, 52, 58–59, 60;
    inspiration for, 51, 62; making of,
    51–53; narration of, 55; norms of juve-
    nile publishing in, 15, 54–57, 61; pos-
    sible inspirations for the name
    "Madeline" in, 61–62; publication of,
    xi, 3, 4, 14, 51–54, 98; reception for,
    53–54; resemblance of earlier works to,
    31–32, 35, 48; *Madeline* series (Viking),
    50–85; as classics, 117–24; formulaic
    approach to, 13, 15–16, 62–63, 79–80;
    offshoots of, 86–88; plots of, 11
Madeline and the Bad Hat, 6, 53, 62,
    68–72, 75; climax of, 71–72; illustra-
    tions in, 70–71
Madeline and the Gypsies, 6, 15, 72–75;
    circus setting for, 75; plot of, 73–74;
    publication of, 62, 72 ; verse narration
    of, 74
Madeline and the Magician (proposed
    book), 84
"Madeline at the Coronation," 63
"Madeline in London," 75; drawing from,
    76 (illus.)
Madeline in London, 6, 75–82, 84;
    Caldecott Committee and, 82; cre-
    ation of, 12, 78–79; kindness to ani-
    mals theme in, 80–81; publication of,
    62; research for, 77–78
Madeline Pop-Up, 116
Madeline's Christmas (book), 15, 62,
    82–85; creation of, 84; critics on, 57;
    differences between other *Madeline*
    books and, 83–84; 1985 edition of,
    84–85; publication of, 62, 82–83
Madeline's Christmas (for *McCall's,* 1956),
    6, 14, 15, 62, 83, 84, 85
"Madeline's Christmas" (for *Good
    Housekeeping,* 1955), 86–87
"Madeline's Christmas" (for *McCall's,*
    1985), 85
Madeline's Christmas in Texas (for Neiman
    Marcus), 6, 14, 15, 86–87, 105

Madeline's House, 116

"Madeline's Rescue," 15, 63

Madeline's Rescue, 13, 63–68; Caldecott Award for, 1, 6, 7, 11, 50, 51, 62, 63, 68, 102; Caldecott Award, acceptance speech for, 11, 12, 51, 58, 60, 64, 65, 69, 109; caricature in, 18; creation of, 12; illustrations in, 66–68; inspiration for, 64–65; plot of, 13; publication of, 53, 62

Mademoiselle (magazine), 110

Marina, 6, 113–15; illustrations in, 115; narration of, 18, 113–14; plot of, 13

Marshall, James, 120–21

Martin, Bill, Jr., 124

Martin, Jay, 5

Massee, May, 3, 14, 15, 20, 59, 81, 82; *The Castle Number Nine,* 20, 38, 41, 42–43, 97; Collection, 128nn3,7, 129n8; dedication of *Madeline and the Gypsies* to, 72; *The Golden Basket* and, 15, 20, 27, 28, 34, 54; *Hansi* and, 15, 20–21, 22, 23, 27, 54, 118; and Bemelmans's letter concerning stories in magazines, 14, 96; *Madeline in London* and, 75, 76–77, 78, 79, 81–82; *Madeline's Christmas* and, 83, 84; rejection of *Madeline* and, 51–53; *Quito Express* and, 15, 20, 45; *Rosebud* and, 92, 93–94; writings about Bemelmans of, 1, 7–8, 9, 23, 27

"Master of All Masters" (folk tale), 37–38

Max and Moritz, 17, 18

Mayer, Mercer, 122

McCall's (magazine): Bemelmans's work in, 14; *Madeline and the Gypsies* in, 15, 73; *Madeline's Christmas* (1956), 6, 14, 15, 62, 83, 84, 85; "Madeline's Christmas" (1985) in, 85

McCloskey, Robert, 23, 26, 121, 123

McCully, Emily Arnold, 122

McGinley, Phyllis, 12, 64, 68

McKissack, Patricia, 122

Mendl, Lady Elsie, 7

Metropolitan Museum of Art, New York, 7

MGM, 5

Miller, Lee, 58

Milwaukee Journal, 3, 16, 18, 19

Minnelli, Vincente, 5

Miss Clavel: fictional predecessor, 31; historical antecedent, 131n16; as security figure, 56; as surrogate mother, 56

Montresor, Beni, 124

Moore, Anne Carroll, 118; collection of, 128n2, 129n31, 131n19; papers of, 126n20

Musée National d'Art Moderne, Paris, 7

Museum of the City of New York, 7

My Life in Art, 6, 112

My War with the United States, 4, 40, 42, 45, 129n28

Nazism, 28, 29, 57

Neiman Marcus, *Madeline's Christmas in Texas* for, 6, 14, 15, 86–87, 105

Ness, Eveline, 121, 124

Newbery Honor Award. *See The Golden Basket*

Newsweek (magazine), 8, 18, 45, 54

New Yorker (magazine), 4, 49, 51, 57–58, 59, 119

New York Herald Tribune, 53, 69, 99

New York Public Library, 22; *see also* Moore, Anne Carroll

New York Times, 9, 27, 45, 54, 57

New York World, 2, 16, 18, 19

Noah (Obey), 4, 27, 31

Noodle (Leaf): Bemelmans's illustrations in, 3, 14, 20, 42, 43–45, 92, 93; popularity of, 44–45

"Noodles, the Trained Seal," 21, 44, 114

"Nosegay," 5, 14, 92, 93; narration of, 18

Now I Lay Me Down to Sleep, 5

Obey, André, 4

"Old Ritz, The," 2–3, 6, 16

"Old Stag and the Tree, The," 106, 109–10

On Board Noah's Ark, 113

Parsley, 6, 105–10; plot of, 13; sale of illustrations from, 6–7; *Woman's Day* edition of, 106, 109–10

Petersham, Maud and Miska, 24, 121, 124

Peterson, Linda Kauffman, 29, 35, 120, 123

Picasso, Pablo, 58, 59
Pinkney, Jerry, 122
Pitz, Henry C., 2, 8, 9
Pomerance, Murray, xi, 4, 16, 21, 27, 54, 69, 94, 102, 106, 114
"Poor Animal!," 69
Provensen, Alice and Martin, 124
Publishers Weekly, 46, 52, 62, 63, 87, 117

Quito Express, 3, 10, 43, 45–49; adult appeal of, 48; drawing from, 47 (illus.); foreign words used in, 47; illustrations in, 48–49, 60; making of, 45–46; norms of juvenile publishing in, 15; plot of, 13, 46–48

Random House, 5, 92
"Randy," 110, 112
Regensburg, Germany, 1–2, 5–6, 10, 28
Rey, H. A., 119
Richards, Olga, 82
Ringgold, Faith, 122
Ritz-Carlton Hotel, New York, 6
Rogow, Lee, 4, 14, 67
Rojankovsky, Feodor, 124
Root, Shelton L., Jr., 68, 109
Rosebud, 5, 14, 92–94
R. R. Bowker, 94
Rylant, Cynthia, 121

Salinas, Marcel, 77, 78, 79, 80
Saturday Evening Post (magazine), 21, 59, 114
Saturday Review (magazine), 4, 8, 67
Scholastic Magazines, 44
Schrank, Joseph, 5
Schwartz, Amy, 121
Sendak, Maurice, 119, 121
Shavit, Zohar, x, 117–18
Shirley Temple Show (television show), 87
"Silly Willy" (comic strip), 3–4, 21, 55, 114
Silly Willy (proposed book), 42, 43, 52
Simon & Schuster, 72; *Fifi* and, 5, 89, 98; Madeline and, 52–53, 54, 98; *Sunshine: A Story about the City of New York* and, 98
Small Beer, 4, 5, 51

Smith, Josephine, 54
Smithsonian Institution, 116
Solt, Marilyn Leathers, 29, 35, 120, 123
Sperry, Armstrong, 25
Spier, Peter, 124
Stanley, Lord Edward, 77
Steig, William, 119
Stein, Gertrude, 121
Street Where the Heart Lies, The, 7
Sunshine: A Story about the City of New York, 5, 6, 10, 96–99; caricature in, 18; narration of, 18
"Sunshine Sunshine Go Away: A Story about the City of New York," 5, 14–15, 96, 102
"Swan Country," 6, 32–34, 125ch1n4

Tale of Two Glimps, A, 5, 94–95
"Tell Them It Was Wonderful," 7
Thery, Jacques, 5
Thompson, Kay, 122
"Thrilling Adventures of Count Bric a Brac," 2–3, 16–19, 21, 55
Thurber, James, 4
Time (magazine), 8, 100
To the One I Love the Best, 7
Touchstones List, 119
Town and Country (magazine), 5, 14, 21, 58, 69, 90, 92, 96
Trelease, Jim, 122
"Trip to Bruges, A," 33, 34–35
trompe l'oeil, 59

Viking Press, 1, 20, 26, 40, 94; acquisition of *Madeline,* 72; *The Castle Number Nine,* 20; format of books for, 62–63; *The Golden Basket* for, 15, 20; *Hansi* for, 15, 20, 25; later books from, 116, 117; *Madeline and the Bad Hat* for, 62; *Madeline and the Gypsies* for, 62, 72; *Madeline in London* for, 62; *Madeline's Christmas* for, 15, 62, 82–83; *Madeline's Rescue* for, 62; *On Board Noah's Ark* for, 113; *Quito Express* for, 15, 20, 43; refusal of *Madeline* by, 51–52; refusal of *Rosebud* by, 94
Vivisection Investigation League, 69
Vogue (magazine), 4, 33, 35, 58

Welcome Home!, 6, 10, 110–13
Welles, Orson, 92
Wells, Rosemary, 120
West, Nathanael, 5
Whalen-Levitt, Peggy, 120
Wheeler, Jody, 84–85
White, E. B., 100
Wiese, Kurt, 3, 23, 24–25, 26, 55, 123
Williams, Vera B., 121–22
Wiseman, Bernie, 119
Woman of My Life, The, 7
Woman's Day (magazine), 106, 109–10
Woman's Home Companion (magazine), 99, 101, 102

Woods, Audrey and Don, 120
World War I, 4
World War II, 5, 6, 25

Yolanda and the Thief (film), 5
Young America (magazine), 3–4, 21, 42, 114
Young Wings (magazine), 10, 12, 32, 33, 53, 65

Zemach, Harve, 124
Zemach, Margot, 124
Zolotow, Charlotte, 121

The Author

Jacqueline Fisher Eastman teaches French, English, and children's literature in Birmingham, Alabama. She earned her B.A. and M.A. in French from Washington University in St. Louis, her M.A. in literature from the University of Illinois in Springfield, and her Ph.D. in English from the University of Alabama. Her writing has appeared in *Children's Literature, Children's Literature Quarterly, Touchstones,* and the *James Joyce Quarterly.* A Lilly Foundation grant from Talladega College, where she was associate professor from 1989 to 1992, enabled her to do research at the Viking Press on Bemelmans's correspondence.

The Editor

Ruth K. MacDonald is associate dean of Bay Path College. She received her B.A. and M.A. in English from the University of Connecticut, her Ph.D. in English from Rutgers University, and her M.B.A. from the University of Texas at El Paso. She is author of the volumes on Louisa May Alcott, Beatrix Potter, and Dr. Seuss in Twayne's United States and English Authors series and of the book *Literature for Children in England and America, 1646–1774* (1982).